CCAT 3 WORKBOOK

Canadian Cognitive Abilities
Test - Grade 3 - Level 9

COPYRIGHT

Copyright © 2025 by Complete Test Preparation Inc.

ALL RIGHTS RESERVED.

No part of this book may be reproduced or transferred in any form or by any means, graphic, electronic, or mechanical, including photocopying, recording, web distribution, taping, or by any information storage retrieval system, without the written permission of the author.

Notice: Complete Test Preparation Inc. makes every reasonable effort to obtain from reliable sources accurate, complete, and timely information about the tests covered in this book. Nevertheless, changes can be made in the tests or the administration of the tests at any time and Complete Test Preparation Inc. makes no representation or warranty, either expressed or implied as to the accuracy, timeliness, or completeness of the information contained in this book. Complete Test Preparation Inc. make no representations or warranties of any kind, express or implied, about the completeness, accuracy, reliability, suitability or availability with respect to the information contained in this document for any purpose. Any reliance you place on such information is therefore strictly at your own risk.

The author(s) shall not be liable for any loss incurred as a consequence of the use and application, directly or indirectly, of any information presented in this work. Sold with the understanding, the author is not engaged in rendering professional services or advice. If advice or expert assistance is required, the services of a competent professional should be sought.

The company, product and service names used in this publication are for identification purposes only. All trademarks and registered trademarks are the property of their respective owners. Complete Test Preparation Inc. is not affiliated with any educational institution.

The producers and administrators of the CCAT are not involved in the production of, and does not endorse this publication.

This title is provided for skill practice only.

We strongly recommend that students check with exam providers for up-to-date information regarding test content.

Version 9.0 February 2025

ISBN: 9781772454598

About Complete Test Preparation Inc.

Why Us?
The Complete Test Preparation Team has been publishing high quality study materials since 2005, with a catalogue of over 145 titles, in English, French and Chinese, as well as curriculum for all levels.

To keep up with the industry changes, we update everything all the time!

And the best part?
With every purchase, you're helping people all over the world improve themselves and their education. So thank you in advance for supporting this mission with us! Together, we are truly making a difference in the lives of those often forgotten by the system.

Charities that we support - https://www.test-preparation.ca/charities-and-non-profits/

You have definitely come to the right place.
If you want to spend your valuable study time where it will help you the most - we've got you covered today and tomorrow.

Published by
Complete Test Preparation Inc.
Victoria BC Canada

Visit us on the web at
https://www.test-preparation.ca
Printed in the USA

Feedback

We welcome your feedback. Email us at feedback@test-preparation.ca with your comments and suggestions. We carefully review all suggestions and often incorporate reader suggestions into upcoming versions. As a Print on Demand Publisher, we update our products frequently.

CONTENTS

8 Introduction

10 Verbal Battery

Vocabulary Quiz 1	14
Answer Key	22
Vocabulary Quiz 2	27
Answer Key	41
Sentence Completion	42
Answer Key	54
Analogies Quiz	60
Answer Key	72
Analogies Quiz 2	74
Answer Key	84

86 Non Verbal Battery

Classification Quiz	87
Answer Key	98
Classification Quiz 2	99
Answer Key	110
Folding Quiz	111
Answer Key	125
Folding Quiz 2	126
Answer Key	137
Figure Matrix Quiz	138
Answer Key	151

Number Analogies Quiz	154	
Answer Key	167	
Number Series Quiz 1	172	
Answer Key	185	
Number Series Quiz 2	188	
Answer Key	199	
Number Puzzles Quiz	202	
Answer Key	212	

213 Taking a Practice Test
    Getting the Most from Practice   214
    After Completing a Practice Test   215

217 Test Preparation Tips

218 How to Answer Multiple Choice

220 Conclusion

INTRODUCTION

Welcome to the Canadian Cognitive Abilities Test Practice Workbook. This resource is designed to help you prepare your child for assessments that evaluate reasoning and problem-solving skills across three key areas:

Verbal Battery: Enhances language comprehension and verbal reasoning abilities.

Quantitative Battery: Develops numerical reasoning and problem-solving skills.

Non-Verbal Battery: Strengthens your ability to understand and analyze visual information.

By working through the practice questions in this workbook with your child, you'll build confidence and proficiency in each area.

Engaging with your Grade 3 child using a practice workbook can be a rewarding experience that reinforces their learning and fosters a positive attitude toward education. Here are some guidelines to help you make the most of this time together:

Establish a Routine: Set aside a consistent time each day for workbook activities. A regular schedule helps your child develop good study habits and provides a sense of structure.

Create a Conducive Environment: Ensure that the study area is quiet, well-lit, and free from distractions. A comfortable space can enhance concentration and make learning more enjoyable.

Review Instructions Together: Before starting an exercise, read the instructions with your child to make sure they understand the questions. Generally it is self explanatory, but reviewing will not hurt! Encourage them to ask questions if anything is unclear.

Encourage Independence: Allow your child to attempt the exercises on their own first. This promotes problem-solving skills and confidence. Offer guidance only when necessary, and praise successful efforts to build self-esteem and confidence.

Discuss Mistakes Positively: Mistakes are learning opportunities. Discuss what went wrong and how to approach similar problems differently in the future. This fosters a growth and problem-solving as well as building confidence.

Use Real-Life Examples: Relate workbook questions to everyday situations. This makes learning relevant and practical.

Celebrate Achievements: Acknowledge your child's progress and successes, no matter how small. Positive reinforcement encourages continued effort and enthusiasm for learning.

These are just a few steps you can take to create a supportive and effective learning environment that complements your child's educational journey.

Verbal Battery Vocabulary I

The Verbal Battery vocabulary section of the Canadian Cognitive Abilities Test (CCAT) for grade 3 evaluates a student's understanding and use of language.

This section includes questions that test vocabulary, verbal analogies, sentence completion, and comprehension skills. Students are asked to demonstrate their knowledge of word meanings, relationships between words, and their ability to follow and interpret written instructions or passages. The goal is to measure a student's linguistic aptitude, which is important for success in various academic subjects.

For example, a vocabulary question might ask students to choose the word that best completes a sentence, while a verbal analogy question might ask them to identify the relationship between pairs of words. Sentence completion questions require students to select the best word to fill in a blank in a sentence, and comprehension questions assess their ability to understand and interpret written passages.

Tips for Answering Vocabulary Questions

1. Understand the Word:

Make sure you know the meaning of the word. For example, if the word is "brave," understand that it means showing courage.

2. Use Context Clues:

Look at the words around the unfamiliar word to help figure out its meaning. For example, in the sentence "The brave knight fought the dragon," the word "fought" can help you understand that "brave" means courageous.

3. Break Down the Word:

Look for smaller words or familiar parts within the word. For example, in the word "unhappy," you can see "happy" and know that "un-" means not, so "unhappy" means not happy.

4. Think of Synonyms and Antonyms:

Think of words that mean the same or the opposite. For example, a synonym for "happy" is "joyful," and an antonym is "sad."

5. Practice with Flashcards:

Use flashcards to review vocabulary words. Write the word on one side and the definition on the other. For example, write "brave" on one side and "showing courage" on the other.

6. Use the Word in a Sentence:

Practice using the word in a sentence to understand its meaning better. For example, "The brave firefighter saved the cat from the tree."

8. Ask for Help:

If you don't understand a word, ask a teacher, parent, or friend for help. For example, if you don't know what "giggle" means, ask someone to explain it to you.

9. Stay Calm and Focused:

Take your time and stay calm when answering questions. For example, if you come across a difficult word, take a deep breath and use the strategies you've learned.

Quiz 1 Answer Sheet

	A	B	C	D	E			A	B	C	D	E
1	○	○	○	○	○		21	○	○	○	○	○
2	○	○	○	○	○		22	○	○	○	○	○
3	○	○	○	○	○		23	○	○	○	○	○
4	○	○	○	○	○		24	○	○	○	○	○
5	○	○	○	○	○		25	○	○	○	○	○
6	○	○	○	○	○		26	○	○	○	○	○
7	○	○	○	○	○		27	○	○	○	○	○
8	○	○	○	○	○		28	○	○	○	○	○
9	○	○	○	○	○		29	○	○	○	○	○
10	○	○	○	○	○		30	○	○	○	○	○
11	○	○	○	○	○
12	○	○	○	○	○
13	○	○	○	○	○
14	○	○	○	○	○
15	○	○	○	○	○
16	○	○	○	○	○
17	○	○	○	○	○
18	○	○	○	○	○
19	○	○	○	○	○
20	○	○	○	○	○

1. What is the opposite of 'hot?'

a. Cold   b. Fast
c. Big   d. Happy

2. Which word means the same as 'tiny?'

a. Wet   b. Huge
c. Small   d. Angry

3. What does 'friendly' mean?

a. Sad   b. Happy

c. Unkind   d. Kind

4. Which word is an opposite of 'big?'

a. Fast   b. Small
c. Blue   d. Hot

5. What does 'quick' mean?

a. Slow   b. Tall

c. Loud   d. Funny

6. What is the opposite of 'happy?'

a. Sad   b. Funny
c. Angry d. Tired

7. Which word means the same as 'big?'

a. Small b. Large
c. Hot   d. Cold

8. Which animal says 'meow?'

a. Dog   b. Cat
c. Bird   d. Cow

9. What is the synonym for 'safe?'

a. Dangerous   b. Secure
c. Brave   c. Fast

10. Which word is an antonym of 'proof?'

a. Evidence   b. Certainty
c. Weakness   d. Support

11. What does 'settle' mean?

a. Agree   b. Move
c. Upset   d. Begin

12 When does 'evening' occur?

a. Morning   b. Afternoon
c. Noon   d. Night

13. What is another word for 'fast?'

a. Slow   b. Quick
c. Long   d. Short

14. Which of the following words means the topmost point?

a. Ocean   b. Peak
c. Scholar   d. Excess

15. Which word refers to a large body of saltwater?

a. Ocean   b. Peak
c. Scholar   d/ Excess

16. Which term is used for a learned or knowledgeable person?

a. Ocean   b. Peak
c. Scholar   d. Excess

17. What does 'excess' mean?

a. Ocean   b. Peak
c. Scholar   d. Excess

18. Which word signifies the highest point reached in a process or activity?

a. Ocean   b. Peak
c. Scholar   d. Excess

19. What is the opposite of 'future?'

a. Now   b. Past
c. Present   d. Tomorrow

20. What word describes something slightly wet or damp?

a. Dry   b. Moist
c. Sunny   d. Cold

21. What does it mean to look back at your reflection in a mirror or water?

a. Reflect b.
c. Jump

b. Turn
c. Run

22. On which planet do we live?

a. Mars
c. Earth

b. Venus
d. Jupiter

23. Which word means a gift?

a. Present
c. Net

b. Label
d. Fair

24. Which word means to jump high in the air?

a. Insect
c. Notice

b. Leap
d. Excite

25. What is a small animal like a bug called?

a. Notice   b. Excite
c. Leap   d. Insect

26. Which word means to see or observe something?

a. Excite   b. Insect
c. Leap   d. Notice

27. What does it mean to feel very happy and eager about something?

a. Insect   b. Excite
c. Leap   d. Notice

28. Which word means to jump quickly forward or upward?

a. Excite
b. Notice
c. Insect
d. Leap

29. What is another word for 'sticker?'

a. Net
b. Fair
c. Label
c. Present

30. If something is just, what word would describe it?

a. Net
b. Fair
c. Label
d. Present

Answer Key

1. A
The opposite of 'hot' is 'cold' because hot refers to something that has a high temperature, while cold refers to something with low or no heat.

2. C
The word 'tiny' means very small in size, so 'small' is the correct choice as it is a synonym for tiny.

3. D
Friendly' means showing kindness or being pleasant, so 'kind' is the correct choice as it relates to being friendly.

4. B
The opposite of 'big' is 'small' as big refers to something large in size and small refers to something not large.

5. A
The word 'quick' means happening or done with great speed, so 'slow' is the opposite of quick because it means not fast.

6. A
The opposite of 'happy' is 'sad'. 'Sad' expresses the feeling of unhappiness or sorrow.

7. B
The word 'large' means the same as 'big', both referring to something of considerable size.

8. B
The animal that says 'meow' is the 'cat'. Cats are known for making this sound.

9. B
The correct answer is 'Secure' as it means free from danger or harm, just like 'Safe'.

10. C
The correct answer is 'Weakness' as it is opposite in meaning to 'Proof', which indicates strength or confirmation.

11. A
The correct answer is 'Agree' as 'Settle' can mean to reach an agreement or resolution.

12. D
The correct answer is 'Night' as 'Evening' is the time between late afternoon and night.

13. B
Another word for 'fast' is 'quick'. 'Quick' describes something done with high speed.

14. B
The correct answer is 'Peak' as it refers to the highest point of something, like a mountain peak.

15. A
The correct answer is 'Ocean.'

16. C
The correct answer is 'Scholar' as it describes someone who has deep knowledge in a particular field.

17. D
The correct answer is 'Excess' which is an amount that is more than necessary or wanted.

18. B
The correct answer is 'Peak' as it reflects the top or climax of something.

19. B
The correct answer is 'Past' because the opposite of future, which means what has happened already, is the past.

20. B
The correct answer is 'Moist' because 'moist' means slightly wet or damp, and the other choices describe different conditions.

21. A
The correct answer is 'Reflect' as it means to look back at your reflection, while the other choices are unrelated actions.

22. C
The correct answer is 'Earth,' the other choices are different planets in our solar system.

23. A
Present' means to give something as a gift.

24. B
The correct answer is 'Leap' as it describes the action of jumping high in the air.

25. D
The correct answer is 'Insect' as it refers to a small animal like a bug.

26. D
The correct answer is 'Notice' as it means to see or observe something.

27. B
The correct answer is 'Excite' as it means to feel very happy and eager about something.

28. D
The correct answer is 'Leap' as it means to jump quickly forward or upward.

29. C
Label' is another word for 'Sticker'. A label is a piece of paper, cloth, or other material attached to an object and showing information about it.

30. B
Fair' is the word that describes something that is just or equitable, treating everyone equally.

Vocabulary Quiz 2

Answer Sheet

	A	B	C	D	E		A	B	C	D	E
1	○	○	○	○	○	21	○	○	○	○	○
2	○	○	○	○	○	22	○	○	○	○	○
3	○	○	○	○	○	23	○	○	○	○	○
4	○	○	○	○	○	24	○	○	○	○	○
5	○	○	○	○	○	25	○	○	○	○	○
6	○	○	○	○	○	26	○	○	○	○	○
7	○	○	○	○	○	27	○	○	○	○	○
8	○	○	○	○	○	28	○	○	○	○	○
9	○	○	○	○	○	29	○	○	○	○	○
10	○	○	○	○	○	30	○	○	○	○	○
11	○	○	○	○	○						
12	○	○	○	○	○						
13	○	○	○	○	○						
14	○	○	○	○	○						
15	○	○	○	○	○						
16	○	○	○	○	○						
17	○	○	○	○	○						
18	○	○	○	○	○						
19	○	○	○	○	○						
20	○	○	○	○	○						

1. An exit or way out is a/an

   a. Door-jamb   b. Egress

   c. Regress   d. Furtherance

2. A warm and kind person is

   a. Seethe   b. Geniality

   c. Desists   d. Predicate

3. A polite and well mannered person is

   a. Chivalrous b. Hilarious

   c. Genteel   d. Governance

4. Something shocking, terrible or wicked is

    a. Pleasantries   b. Heinous

    c. Shrewd   d. Provencal

5. Something perfect, with no faults or errors is

    a. Impeccable   b. Formidable

    c. Genteel   d. Disputation

6. Quick and light in movement is

    a. Quickest   b. Nimble

    c. Rapacious   d. Perspicuities

7. A loud unpleasant noise is a/an

    a. Nosy   b. Racket

    c. Ravage d. Noisome

8. Someone appearing weak or pale is

    a. Pallid   b. Palliative

    c. Deviant d. Expatiate

9. A question or inquiry is a

    a. Cite   b. Query

    c. Linger d. Gibe

10. To move back or away is to

    a. Implicate   b. Oscillate

    c. Recede   d. Meander

11. Complete agreement or harmony is

    a. Ambiguous   b. Unanimous

    c. Adulate   d. Incredulous

12. Friendship; peaceful harmony is

    a. Amity   b. Palliative

    c. Chivalrous   d. Nebulous

13. Commonplace; tired or petty is

    a. Obdurate   b. Distraught

    c. Banal   d. Meticulous

14. To shake or wave, is to

    a. Occilate   b. Osculate

    c. Brandish   d. Avert

15. Fearless, intrepid or bold is

    a. Meticulous   b. Dauntless

    c. Ambiguous   d. Shrivel

16. To cause or inflict harm or injury is to

    a. Wreck   b. Mandible

    c. Tremulous   d. Juxtapose

17. A strong fear of strangers is

    a. Xenophobia   b. Agoraphobia

    c. Frightful   d. Genteel

18. The highest point, highest state or peak is the

    a. Towering   b. Flickers

    c. Zenith   d. Grouse

19. A light wind or gentle breeze is called a

    a. Sea-breeze   b. Scuttle

    c. Zephyr   d. Freight

20. Which of the following best defines the word "accident?"

    a. A planned event

    b. An unintentional event causing damage or injury

    c. A joyful celebration

    d. A regular occurrence

21. What does the "arrive" mean?

a. To depart from a place

b. To reach a destination

c. To get lost

d. To cancel a trip

22. An "atlas" is

a. A type of flower

b. A collection of maps

c. A historical artifact

d. A medical tool

23. To pay "attention" means to:

a. Ignore something

b. Observe or listen carefully

c. Speak loudly

d. Write a letter

24. An "award" is

a. A punishment for wrongdoing

b. A game played by children

c. A prize given for achievement

d. A routine task

25. Which of the following best defines the word "base?"

a. The top part of something

b. The bottom support of something

c. A type of fruit

d. A measure of length

26. What does "beach" mean?

a. A mountain range

b. A desert area

c. A shore of a body of water covered with sand or pebbles

d. A dense forest

27. A "blast" is

   a. A gentle breeze

   b. An explosion or strong burst of air

   c. A type of flower

   d. A musical instrument

28. The "brain" is:

   a. A computer program

   b. A type of plant

   c. The organ in the head that controls thought and feeling

   d. A piece of furniture

29. Which of the following best defines the word "brave?"

a. Showing fear in dangerous situations

b. Running away from challenges

c. Showing courage in the face of fear or danger

d. Avoiding difficult tasks

30. What does "calf" mean?

a. A type of bird

b. A young cow

c. A part of a tree

d. A type of shoe

ANSWER KEY

1. B
2. B
3. C
4. B
5. A
6. B
7. B
8. A
9. B
10. B
11. B
12. A
13. C
14. C
15. B
16. A
17. A
18. C
19. C
20. B
21. B
22. B
23. B
24. C
25. B
26. C
27. B
28. C
29. C
30. B

Verbal Battery - Sentence Completion

The CCAT Verbal Battery - Sentence Completion section is designed to evaluate your ability to understand and complete sentences based on context and word usage.

The examiner or proctor will read out a sentence with one missing word. Candidates must listen to determine what the sentence is trying to communicate, then select the best answer from the options given.

The questions in the first half contain the text and audio in one file - there is a 10 second pause between questions. Questions in the second half only have the audio.

Example: She _____ to the store to buy groceries.

Objective: Evaluate vocabulary knowledge, contextual understanding, and the ability to integrate information to form coherent sentences.
Verbal Classification:

What is a QR Code?

A QR code looks like a barcode and it's used as a shortcut to link to content online using your phone's camera, saving you from typing lengthy addresses into your mobile browser.

Audio for Questions 1 - 15

https://test-preparation.ca/audio/CCATSC-1.mp3

Quiz 1 Answer Sheet

	A	B	C	D	E		A	B	C	D	E
1	○	○	○	○	○	21	○	○	○	○	○
2	○	○	○	○	○	22	○	○	○	○	○
3	○	○	○	○	○	23	○	○	○	○	○
4	○	○	○	○	○	24	○	○	○	○	○
5	○	○	○	○	○	25	○	○	○	○	○
6	○	○	○	○	○						
7	○	○	○	○	○						
8	○	○	○	○	○						
9	○	○	○	○	○						
10	○	○	○	○	○						
11	○	○	○	○	○						
12	○	○	○	○	○						
13	○	○	○	○	○						
14	○	○	○	○	○						
15	○	○	○	○	○						
16	○	○	○	○	○						
17	○	○	○	○	○						
18	○	○	○	○	○						
19	○	○	○	○	○						
20	○	○	○	○	○						

1. Tommy can _____ very fast.

    a. forget   b. drink

    c. run   d. sleep

2. Birds use their _____ to fly.

    a. feet   b. wings

    c. hands   d. tail

3. The dog likes to chase the _____.

    a. cat   b. fence

    c. cloud   d. tree

4. Jenny drinks milk from a _____.

    a. bottle   b. spoon

    c. fork   d. plate

5. The tree has many _____.

    a. houses   b. leaves

    c. books   d. chairs

6. A fish lives in the _____.

    a. tree   b. sky

    c. water   d. grass

7. Mary likes to read a _____ before bed.

    a. game   b. book

    c. song   d. toy

8. The sky is _____ at night.

    a. blue   b. green

    c. light   d. dark

9. We put on a _____ when it is cold outside.

    a. blanket   b. coat

    c. pants   d. swimsuit

10. The teacher writes on the _____.

    a. blackboard   b. floor

    c. ceiling   d. door

11. We eat breakfast in the _____.

    a. morning   b. afternoon

    c. evening   d. night

12. I like to play with my ____.

    a. dog   b. cat

    c. fish   d. bird

13. **The sky is blue during the ____.**

    a. day   b. night

    c. rain   d. snow

14. **I brush my ____ every morning.**

    a. hair   b. teeth

    c. shoes d. book

15. **I go to school by ____.**

    a. bus   b. boat

    c. bike   d. helicopter

Part 2

Audio for questions 16 - 26

https://test-preparation.ca/audio/CCATSC-2.mp3

16.

a. vegetables b. candy

c. pizza d. ice cream

17.
- a. blue
- b. chair
- c. cat
- d. ball

18.
- a. sky
- b. ocean
- c. kitchen
- d. playground

19.
- a. horse
- b. moon
- c. flower
- d. tree

20.
- a. banana
- b. stars
- c. shoe
- d. book

21.

    a. water   b. cake

    c. bird   d. desk

22.

    a. table   b. park

    c. cloud   d. sun

23.

    a. toys   b. books

    c. clothes   d. shoes

24.

    a. Red   b. Blue

    c. Green   d. Yellow

25.

a. flowers b. trees

c. rocks d. sand

Answer Key

1. C
Run is the best choice. Tommy can run very fast.

2. B
Birds use their wings to fly.

3. A
The dog likes to chase the cat.

4. A
Jenny drinks milk from a bottle.

5. B
The tree has many leaves.

6. C
A fish lives in the water.

7. B
Mary likes to read a book before bed.

8. D
The sky is dark at night.

9. B
We put on a coat when it is cold outside.

10. A
The teacher writes on the blackboard.

11. A
We eat breakfast in the morning.

12. A
The correct answer is 'dog' because the sentence indicates a personal preference, and 'dog' fits the context of playing.

13. A
The correct answer is 'day' as the sentence sets up a contrast between day and night, implying the sky color during daytime.

14. B
The correct answer is 'teeth' because the action
of brushing in the morning usually refers to dental hygiene.

15. A
The correct answer is 'bus' as it is a common mode of transportation for students to reach school.

16. A
The correct answer is 'vegetables' since they are commonly associated with maintaining good health.

17. A
The correct answer is A. blue because the question asks about a color, and 'blue' is a color.

18. C
The correct answer is C. kitchen because the question relates to where meals are typically prepared, and the kitchen is the correct place for cooking.

19. A
The correct answer is 'horse' because it is something that can be played with and fits the sentence context.

20. B
The correct answer is 'stars' as it is something one can watch in the evening and matches the context of the sentence.

21. B
The correct answer is 'cake' because it is something that grandmothers commonly bake and is a type of food.

22. B
The correct answer is 'park' as it is a common place for children to play and fits the sentence context.

23. A
The correct answer is 'toys' as it is a common activity for children to play with toys after school.

24. B
The correct answer is 'Blue' as it is stated that the person's favorite color is mentioned in the sentence.

25. A
The correct answer is 'flowers' as they require watering to stay healthy and bloom.

Verbal Analogies

The Verbal Battery specifically measures a student's ability to understand and reason using concepts, assessing verbal reasoning, comprehension, and the capacity to use language in problem-solving tasks.

Components of the Verbal Battery

Verbal Analogies:

Description: Students are presented with pairs of words that share a relationship. They must identify a similar relationship between a new pair of words.

Example: Dog is to Puppy as Cat is to _____.

Objective: Assess the ability to discern relationships between words and apply logical reasoning to identify analogous pairs.

Tips for Answering

Read Carefully: Ensure you understand each word and the relationships presented. Misinterpretation can lead to incorrect answers.

Identify Relationships: Determine the relationship between the first pair of words before selecting the analogous pair.

Quiz 1 Answer Sheet

	A B C D E		A B C D E
1	○ ○ ○ ○ ○	21	○ ○ ○ ○ ○
2	○ ○ ○ ○ ○	22	○ ○ ○ ○ ○
3	○ ○ ○ ○ ○	23	○ ○ ○ ○ ○
4	○ ○ ○ ○ ○	24	○ ○ ○ ○ ○
5	○ ○ ○ ○ ○	25	○ ○ ○ ○ ○
6	○ ○ ○ ○ ○	26	○ ○ ○ ○ ○
7	○ ○ ○ ○ ○	27	○ ○ ○ ○ ○
8	○ ○ ○ ○ ○	28	○ ○ ○ ○ ○
9	○ ○ ○ ○ ○	29	○ ○ ○ ○ ○
10	○ ○ ○ ○ ○	30	○ ○ ○ ○ ○
11	○ ○ ○ ○ ○		
12	○ ○ ○ ○ ○		
13	○ ○ ○ ○ ○		
14	○ ○ ○ ○ ○		
15	○ ○ ○ ○ ○		
16	○ ○ ○ ○ ○		
17	○ ○ ○ ○ ○		
18	○ ○ ○ ○ ○		
19	○ ○ ○ ○ ○		
20	○ ○ ○ ○ ○		

Analogies

Instructions: Choose the option with the same relationship.

1. Pork : Pig :: Beef :

a. Herd   b. Farmer

c. Cow   d. Lamb

2. Fruit : Banana :: Mammal :

a. Cow   b. Snake

c. Fish   d. Sparrow

3. Slumber : Sleep :: Bog :

a. Dream   b. Foray

c. Swamp   d. Night

4. Zoology : Animals

    a. Ecology : Pollution

    b. Botany : Plants

    c. Chemistry : Atoms

    d. History : People

5. Child : Human

    a. Dog : Pet

    b. Kitten : Cat

    c. Cow : Milk

    d. Bird : Robin

6. Wax : Candle

    a. Ink : Pen

    b. Clay : Bowl

    c. String : Kite

    d. Liquid : Cup

7. Which word does not belong with the others?

    a. Jet   b. Float Plane

    c. Kite   d. Biplane

8. Which of the following does not belong?

    a. Number   b. Denominate

    c. Numerate   d. Figure

9. Which of the following does not belong?

    a. Abc   b. bCD

    c. Nmo   d. Pqr

10. Which of the following does not belong?

    a. CD   b. OP

    c. LM   d. BD

11. Which of the following does not belong?

    a. 121212　　b. 141414

    c. 151415　　d. 292929

12. Which of the following does not belong?

    a. 246　　b. 123

    c. 468　　d. 24

13. Which of the following does not belong?

    a. aBCd　　b. lMNo

    c. PQrs　　d. tUVw

14. Which of the following does not belong?

a. ABCD   b. JKLM

c. PQRS   d. WXYZ

15. Which of the following does not belong?

a. BBCCDDEE   b. LLMMNNOO

c. HHIIJJKK   d. RRSSTTUU

16. Which of the following does not belong?

a. def   b. nop

c. tuv   d. lmn

17. Which of the following does not belong?

    a. Argue   b. Talk

    c. Dispute   d. Contest

18. Winner : Champion :: Sheen :

    a. Shimmer   b. Dark

    c. Sweet   d. Garbage

19. Frog : Amphibian :: Snake :

    a. Reptile   b. Bacteria

    c. Protozoan d. Mammal

20. Petal : Flower :: Fur

   a. Coat   b. Warm

   c. Woman   d. Rabbit

21. Present : Birthday :: Reward :

   a. Accomplishment   b. Medal

   c. Acceptance   d. Cash

22. Shovel : Dig :: Scissors :

   a. Scoop   b. Carry

   c. Snip   d. Rip

23. Finger : Hand :: Leg :

   a. Body   b. Foot

   c. Toe   d. Hip

24. Sleep in : Late :: Skip breakfast :

a. Hungry   b. Early

c. Lunch   d. Dinner

25. Circle : Sphere :: Square :

a. Triangle   b. Oval

c. Half Circle   d. Cube

26. Orange : Fruit :: Carrot:

a. Vegetable   b. Bean

c. Food   d. Apple

27. Which of the following does not belong?

    a. ddeeffgg   b. fgghhii

    c. nnooppqq   d. ttuuvvww

28. Which of the following does not belong?

    a. 11223344   b. 33445566

    c. 33455666   d. 44556677

29. Which of the following does not belong?

    a. mNo   b. pQr

    c. Stu   d. xYz

30. Which of the following does not belong?

a. abcabc

b. defdef

c. ghihij

d. mnomno

Answer Key

1. C
2. A
3. C
4. B
5. B
6. B
7. C
8. D
9. B
10. D
11. C
12. B
13. C
14. B
15. C
16. D
17. B
18. A
19. A
20. D
21. A
22. C
23. A
24. A
25. D
26. A
27. B
28. C
29. C
30. C

Quiz 2 Answer Sheet

	A	B	C	D	E		A	B	C	D	E
1	○	○	○	○	○	21	○	○	○	○	○
2	○	○	○	○	○	22	○	○	○	○	○
3	○	○	○	○	○	23	○	○	○	○	○
4	○	○	○	○	○	24	○	○	○	○	○
5	○	○	○	○	○	25	○	○	○	○	○
6	○	○	○	○	○	26	○	○	○	○	○
7	○	○	○	○	○	27	○	○	○	○	○
8	○	○	○	○	○	28	○	○	○	○	○
9	○	○	○	○	○	29	○	○	○	○	○
10	○	○	○	○	○	30	○	○	○	○	○
11	○	○	○	○	○						
12	○	○	○	○	○						
13	○	○	○	○	○						
14	○	○	○	○	○						
15	○	○	○	○	○						
16	○	○	○	○	○						
17	○	○	○	○	○						
18	○	○	○	○	○						
19	○	○	○	○	○						
20	○	○	○	○	○						

1. Which of the following does not belong?

    a. Dog   b. Wolf

    c. Terrier   d. Cougar

2. Which of the following does not belong?

    a. DDDdddEEE   b. MMMoooPPP

    c. GGGhhhIII   d. JJJkkkLLL

3. Which of the following does not belong?

    a. cde   b. mno

    c. stu   d. abc

4. Which of the following does not belong?

    a. 446688　　b. 224466

    c. 336699　　d. 66881010

5. Which of the following does not belong?

    a. Assume　　b. Certain

    c. Sure　　　d. Positive

6. Which of the following does not belong?

    a. MnOp　　b. AbCD

    c. QrSt　　　d. WxYz

7. Which of the following does not belong?

    a. Look   b. See

    c. Perceive   d. Surmise

8. Which of the following does not belong?

    a. Count   b. Number

    c. Add up   d. List

9. Which of the following does not belong?

    a. Secure   b. Discard

    c. Throw out   d. Abandon

10. PETAL is to FLOWER as FUR is to

   a. Coat   b. Warm

   c. Woman   d. Rabbit

11. PRESENT is to BIRTHDAY as REWARD is to

   a. Accomplishment   b. Medal

   c. Acceptance   d. Cash

12. SHOVEL is to DIG as SCISSORS is to

   a. Scoop   b. Carry

   c. Snip   d. Rip

13. FINGER is to HAND as LEG is to

    a. Body   b. Foot

    c. Toe   d. Hip

14. SLEEP IN is to LATE as SKIP BREAKFAST is

    a. Hungry   b. Early

    c. Lunch   d. Dinner

15. CIRCLE is to SPHERE as SQUARE is to   Triangle

    a. Oval   b. Half

    c. Circle   d. Cube

16. ORANGE is to FRUIT as CARROT is to

    a. Vegetable   b. Bean

    c. Food   d. Apple

17. PAPER is to LIGHT as LEAD is to

    a. Grey   b. Solid

    c. Thick   d. Heavy

18. STEEL is to CAR as GLASS is to

    a. Pane   b. Window

    c. Transparent   d. Fragile

19. FOUR-LEAF CLOVER is to LUCK as CROSS is to

    a. Christianity   b. Religion

    c. Wood   d. Tree

20. NEST is to BIRD as CAVE is to

    a. Bear   b. Petal

    c. House   d. Dog

21. TEACHER is to SCHOOL as WAITRESS is to

    a. Office   b. Coffee shop

    c. Customer   d. Student

22. PEBBLE is to BOULDER as POND is to

    a. Ocean   b. River

    c. Drop   d. Rapids

23. DOG is to POODLE as SHARK is to

    a. Great White   b. Dolphin

    c. Whale   d. Fish

24. FOX is to CHICKEN as CAT is to

    a. Rabbit   b. Mouse

    c. Cat   d. Hen

25. LAWYER is to TRIAL as DOCTOR is to

    a. Patient   b. Business man

    c. Operation   d. Nurse

26. EAT is to FAT as BREATHE is to

    a. Inhale   b. Live

    c. Drink   d. Talk

27. MELT is to LIQUID as FREEZE is to

    a. Ice   b. Condense

    c. Solid   d. Stream

28. CLOCK is to TIME as THERMOMETER is to

    a. Heat   b. Radiation

    c. Energy   d. Temperature

29. CAR is to GARAGE as PLANE is to

    a. Depot   b. Port

    c. Hanger   d. Harbour

30. ACTING is to THEATER as GAMBLING is to

    a. Gym   b. Bar

    c. Club   d. Casino

Answer Key

1. D
2. B
3. D
4. C
5. A
6. B
7. D
8. D
9. A
10. D
11. A
12. C
13. A
14. A
15. D
16. A
17. D
18. B
19. A
20. A
21. B
22. A
23. A
24. B
25. C
26. B
27. C
28. D
29. C
30. D

Answer Sheet

	A	B	C	D
1	○	○	○	○
2	○	○	○	○
3	○	○	○	○
4	○	○	○	○
5	○	○	○	○
6	○	○	○	○
7	○	○	○	○
8	○	○	○	○
9	○	○	○	○
10	○	○	○	○
11	○	○	○	○
12	○	○	○	○
13	○	○	○	○
14	○	○	○	○
15	○	○	○	○
16	○	○	○	○
17	○	○	○	○
18	○	○	○	○
19	○	○	○	○
20	○	○	○	○

NON VERBAL BATTERY

The Non-Verbal Battery evaluates reasoning and problem-solving skills through geometric shapes and figures, independent of language abilities.

Description: In this section, students are presented with sets of geometric figures that share a common attribute. The task is to identify the characteristic linking the given figures and select the option that best fits the same category.

Objective: Assess the ability to recognize patterns, categorize visual information, and apply logical reasoning without relying on verbal cues.

CLASSIFICATION

Instructions and Tips for Answering Figure Classification Questions:

Observe Common Features:

Examine the given figures to identify shared attributes, such as shape, size, color, shading, or patterns.

Analyze Answer Options:

Compare each choice against the identified common feature to determine which one aligns with the given set.

Eliminate Irrelevant Choices:

Cross out and eliminate options that do not share the common feature, narrowing down potential correct answers.

Consider Multiple Attributes:

Some questions may involve more than one common feature. Ensure all identified attributes are considered when selecting the answer.

Practice Visualizing:
Practice visualizing geometric figures and patterns to become familiar with different classifications.

1. Select the choice that does not belong.

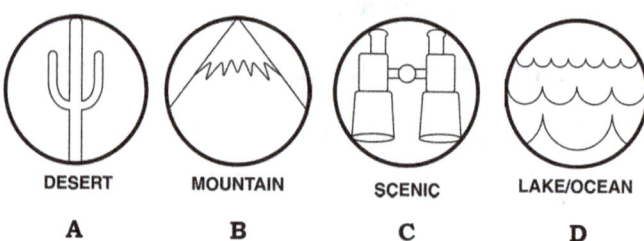

2. Select the choice that does not belong.

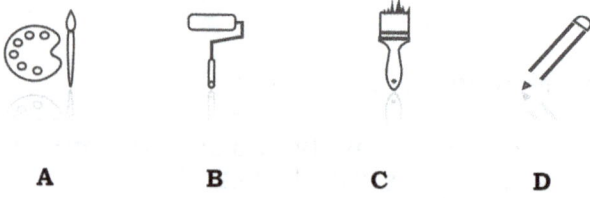

3. Select the choice that does not belong.

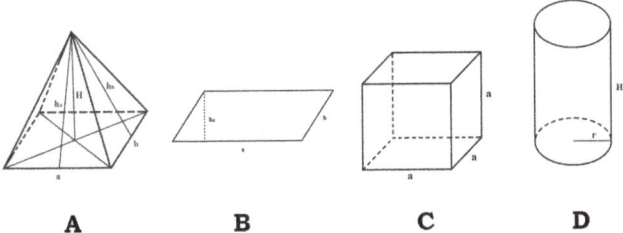

A B C D

4. Select the choice that does not belong.

AB MN PR XY
   A   B   C   D

5. Select the choice that does not belong.

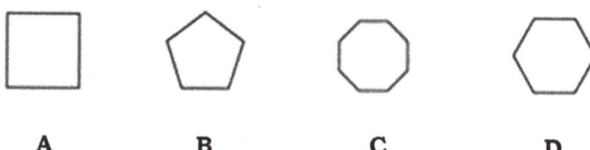

6. Select the choice that does not belong.

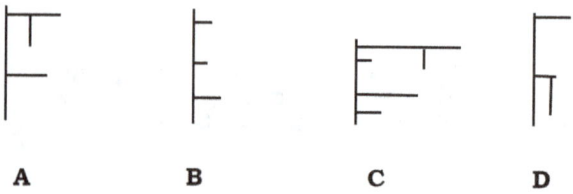

7. Select the choice that does not belong.

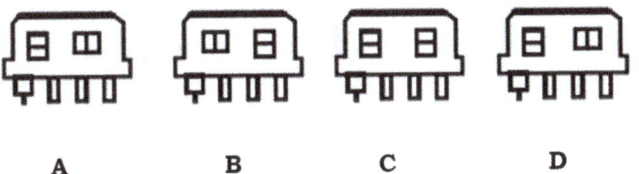

   A   B   C   D

8. Select the choice that does not belong.

   A   B   C   D

9. Select the choice that does not belong.

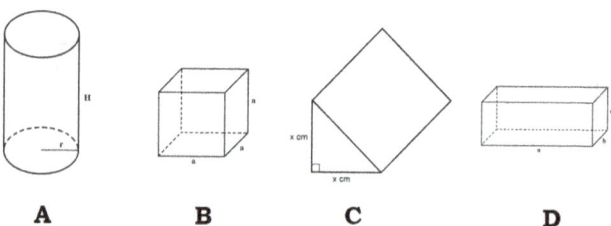

10. Select the choice that does not belong.

11. Select the choice that does not belong.

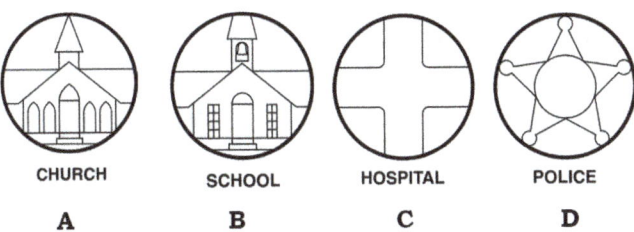

12. Select the choice that does not belong.

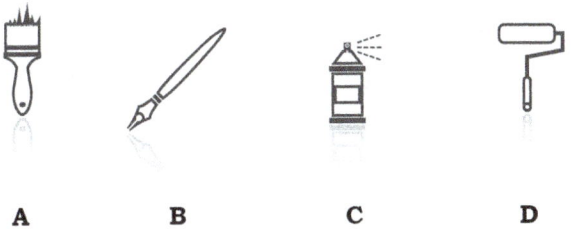

13. Select the choice that does not belong.

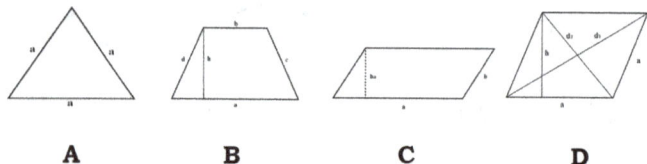

14. Select the choice that does not belong.

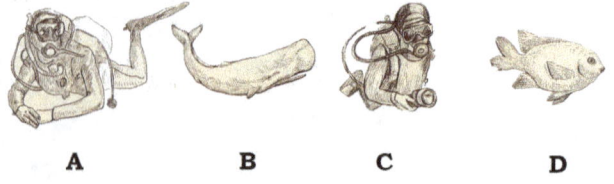

15. Select the choice that does not belong.

25　68　85　40
　A　　B　　C　　D

16. Select the choice that does not belong.

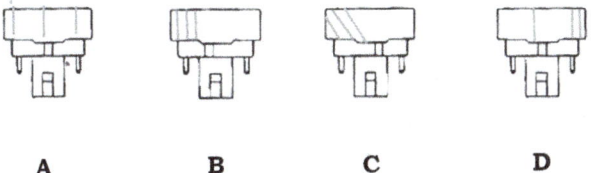

　A　　B　　C　　D

17. Select the choice that does not belong.

18. Select the choice that does not belong.

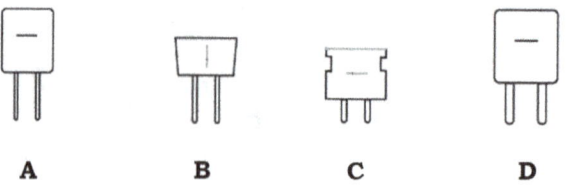

19. **Select the choice that does not belong.**

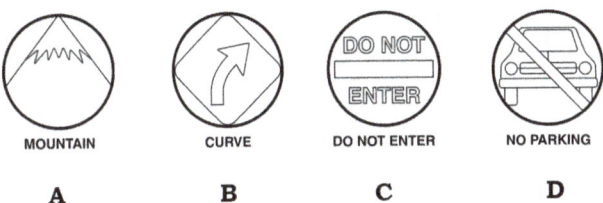

20. **Select the choice that does not belong.**

Answer Key

1. C
2. D
3. B
4. C
5. B
6. C
7. D
8. C
9. A
10. A
11. D
12. B
13. A
14. D
15. B
16. D
17. D
18. B
19. A
20. A

Verbal Battery -

Classification Quiz 2

1. Which of the following does not belong?

   a. Dog
   b. Wolf
   c. Terrier
   d. Cougar

2. Which of the following does not belong?

   a. DDDdddEEE
   b. MMMoooPPP
   c. GGGhhhIII
   d. JJJkkkLLL

3. Which of the following does not belong?

   a. cde
   b. mno
   c. stu
   d. abc

4. Which of the following does not belong?

    a. 446688   b. 224466

    c. 336699   d. 66881010

5. Which of the following does not belong?

    a. Assume   b. Certain

    c. Sure   d. Positive

6. Which of the following does not belong?

    a. MnOp   b. AbCD

    c. QrSt   d. WxYz

7. Which of the following does not belong?

    a. Look   b. See

    c. Perceive   d. Surmise

8. Which of the following does not belong?

    a. Count   b. Number

    c. Add up   d. List

9. Which of the following does not belong?

    a. Secure   b. Discard

    c. Throw out   d. Abandon

10. PETAL is to FLOWER as FUR is to

    a. Coat   b. Warm

    c. Woman   d. Rabbit

11. PRESENT is to BIRTHDAY as REWARD is to

    a. Accomplishment   b. Medal

    c. Acceptance   d. Cash

12. SHOVEL is to DIG as SCISSORS is to

    a. Scoop   b. Carry

    c. Snip   d. Rip

13. FINGER is to HAND as LEG is to

    a. Body   b. Foot

    c. Toe   d. Hip

14. SLEEP IN is to LATE as SKIP BREAKFAST is

    a. Hungy   b. Early

    c. Lunch   d. Dinner

15. CIRCLE is to SPHERE as SQUARE is to

    a. Triangle   b. Oval

    c. Half Circle   d. Cube

16. ORANGE is to FRUIT as CARROT is to

    a. Vegetable   b. Bean

    c. Food   d. Apple

17. PAPER is to LIGHT as LEAD is to

    a. Grey   b. Solid

    c. Thick   d. Heavy

18. STEEL is to CAR as GLASS is to

    a. Pane   b. Window

    c. Transparent   d. Fragile

19. FOUR-LEAF CLOVER is to LUCK as CROSS is to

    a. Christianity   b. Religion

    c. Wood   d. Tree

20. NEST is to BIRD as CAVE is to

    a. Bear   b. Petal

    c. House   d. Dog

21. TEACHER is to SCHOOL as WAITRESS is to

    a. Office   b. Coffee shop

    c. Customer   d. Student

22. PEBBLE is to BOULDER as POND is to

    a. Ocean   b. River

    c. Drop   d. Rapids

23. DOG is to POODLE as SHARK is to

    a. Great White   b. Dolphin

    c. Whale   d. Fish

24. FOX is to CHICKEN as CAT is to

    a. Rabbit   b. Mouse

    c. Cat   d. Hen

25. LAWYER is to TRIAL as DOCTOR is to

    a. Patient   b. Business man

    c. Operation   d. Nurse

26. EAT is to FAT as BREATHE is to

    a. Inhale   b. Live

    c. Drink   d. Talk

27. MELT is to LIQUID as FREEZE is to

    a. Ice   b. Condense

    c. Solid   d. Stream

28. CLOCK is to TIME as THERMOMETER is to

    a. Heat   b. Radiation

    c. Energy   d. Temperature

29. CAR is to GARAGE as PLANE is to

    a. Depot   b. Port

    c. Hanger d. Harbour

30. ACTING is to THEATER as GAMBLING is to

    a. Gym   b. Bar

    c. Club   d. Casino

Answer Key

1. D
2. B
3. D
4. C
5. A
6. B
7. D
8. D
9. A
10. D
11. A
12. C
13. A
14. A
15. D
16. A
17. D
18. B
19. A
20. A
21. B
22. A
23. A
24. B
25. C
26. B
27. C
28. D
29. C
30. D

Non Verbal Battery - Folding

The folding questions of the Non-Verbal Battery, you are shown a series of images that represent how a piece of paper is unfolded. Your task is to determine what the paper will look when it is folded.

Folding questions often test your spatial reasoning skills by asking you to visualize how a two-dimensional shape folds into a three-dimensional object. These questions can appear challenging, but with a clear strategy, you can approach them confidently. Follow these steps:

1. Understand the Question
Carefully read the instructions and review the shape presented and the choices.

Identify the folds or lines on the two-dimensional diagram. These lines indicate where the paper will be folded.

2. Visualize the Fold
Imagine folding the shape along the lines step by step.
Pay attention to how each section aligns with the section next to it after folding.

3. Look for Clues

- **Matching Edges:** Check for patterns, symbols, or colors that should align when folded.

- **Shaded or Marked Areas:** Notice shaded or marked areas that provide hints about the resulting shape.

- **Position of Tabs or Flaps:** Consider which sections will become edges, faces, or corners.

Use your fingers to "trace" folds mentally, imagining how the shape will form.

4. Eliminate Wrong Answers
This is the best strategy for any multiple choice question. Compare the given answer choices to your visualization. Eliminate the most obviously incorrect answers.

Focus on details like symmetry, alignment, and matching edges to narrow down your choices.

Discard options that:

- Mis-align patterns or symbols.

- Have the wrong shape or dimensions.

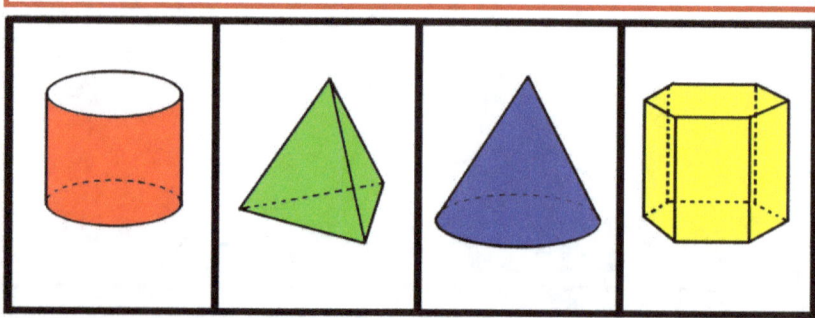

- Show impossible configurations (e.g., overlapping faces or incorrect angles).

6. Sketch if Allowed
If the test permits scratch paper, sketch the folds to better visualize the 3D object.

Mark which parts of the flat diagram correspond to specific sides of the folded shape.

7. Double-Check Your Choice
Revisit the question and ensure your answer matches the expected folded shape. Good advice for any type of question on a test.

Confirm the chosen option aligns with all visible folds, patterns, and angles.

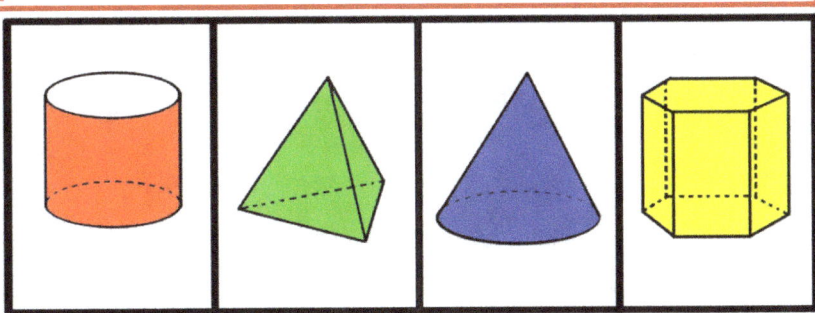

Folding Answer Sheet - Quiz 1

	A	B	C	D
1	○	○	○	○
2	○	○	○	○
3	○	○	○	○
4	○	○	○	○
5	○	○	○	○
6	○	○	○	○
7	○	○	○	○
8	○	○	○	○
9	○	○	○	○
10	○	○	○	○
11	○	○	○	○
12	○	○	○	○
13	○	○	○	○
14	○	○	○	○
15	○	○	○	○
16	○	○	○	○
17	○	○	○	○
18	○	○	○	○
19	○	○	○	○
20	○	○	○	○

1. When the two longest sides touch what will the shape be?

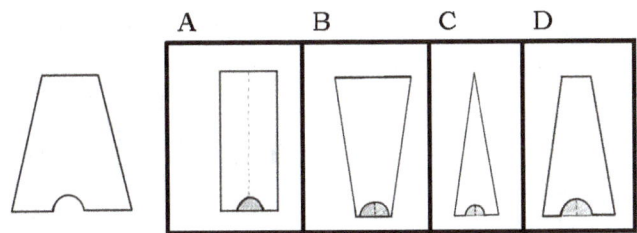

2. When folded, what pattern is possible?

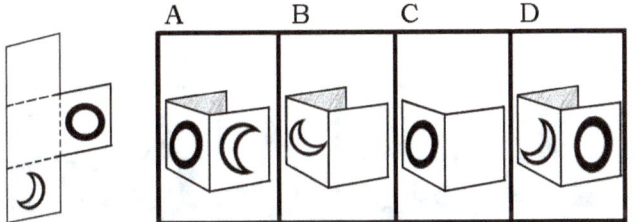

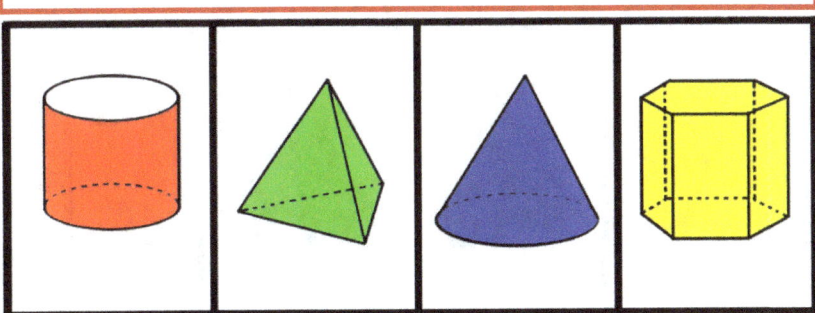

3. When folded into a loop, what will the strip of paper look like?

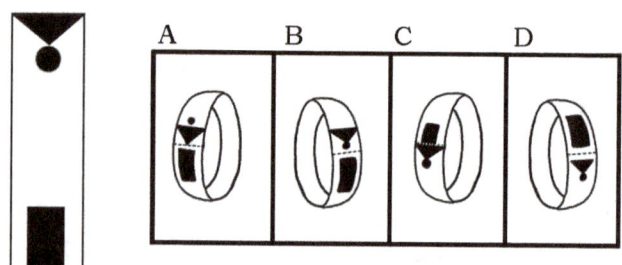

4. Which of the choices is the same pattern at a different angle?

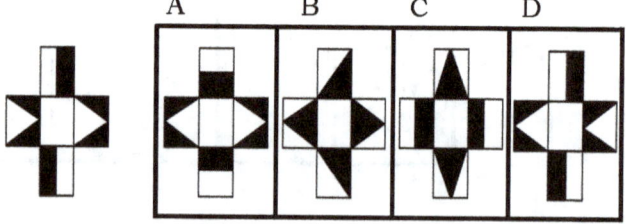

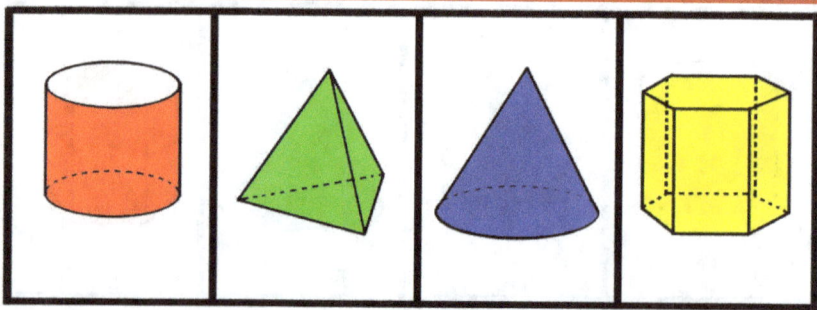

5. When put together, what 3-dimensional shape will you get?

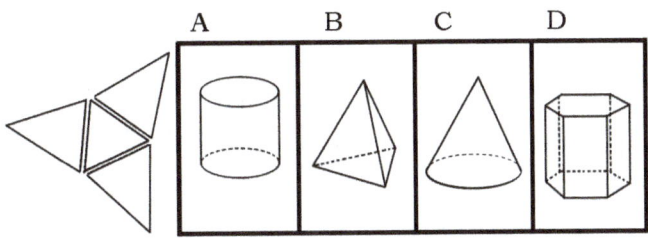

6. When folded, what pattern is possible?

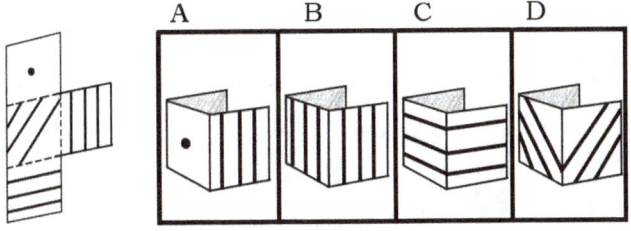

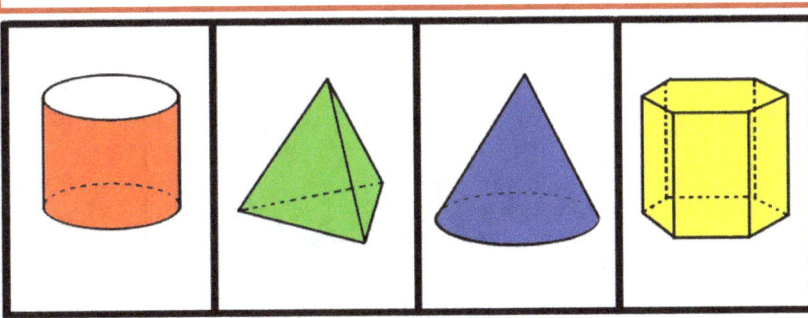

7. When folded into a loop, what will the strip of paper look like?

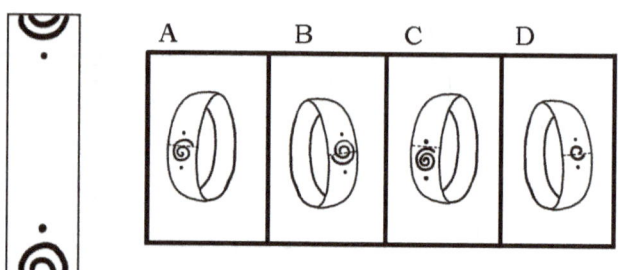

8. Which of the choices is the same pattern at a different angle?

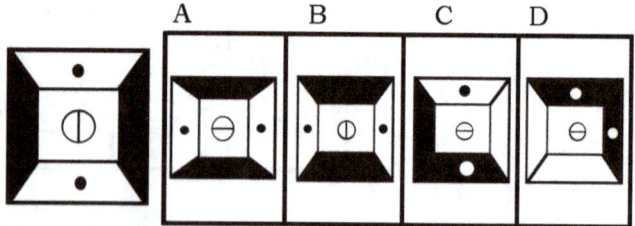

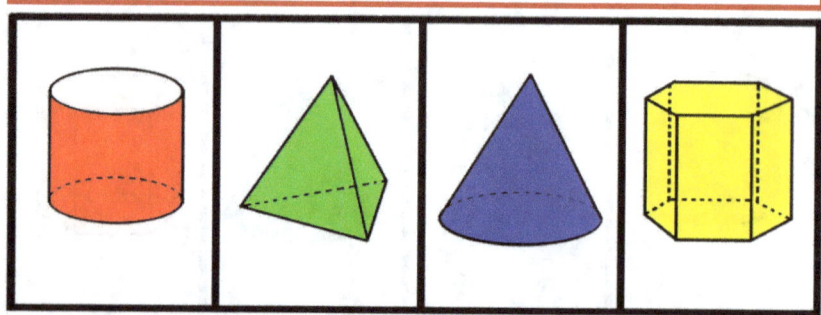

9. When folded, which shape will you get?

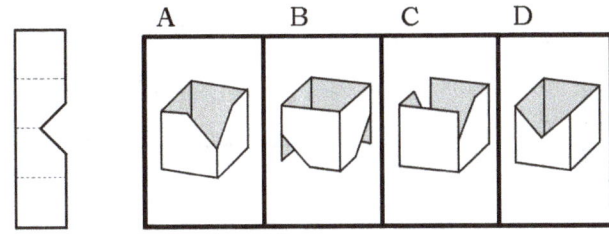

10. When folded, what pattern is possible?

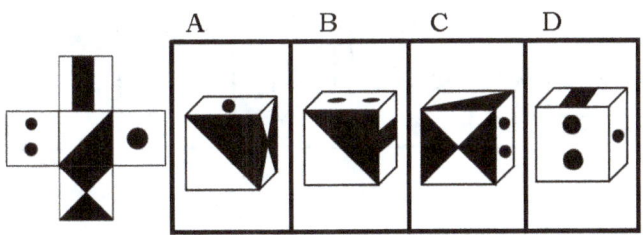

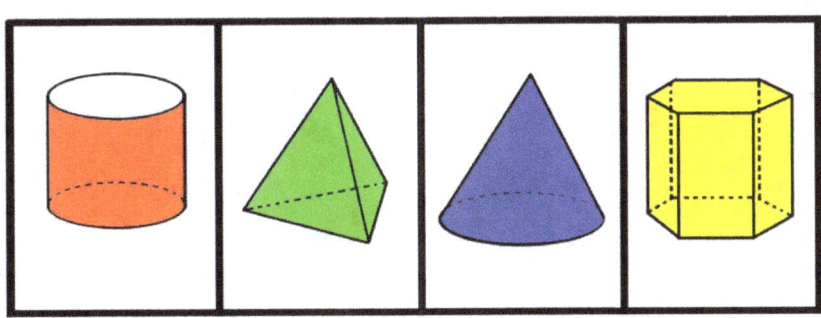

11. When folded, which shape is possible?

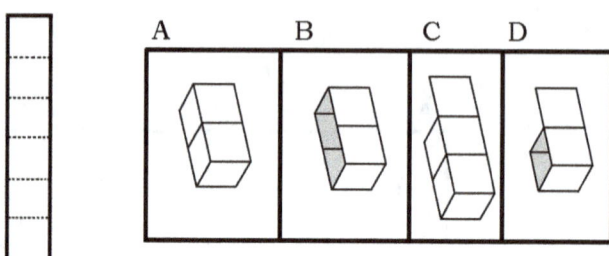

12. When folded, what pattern is possible?

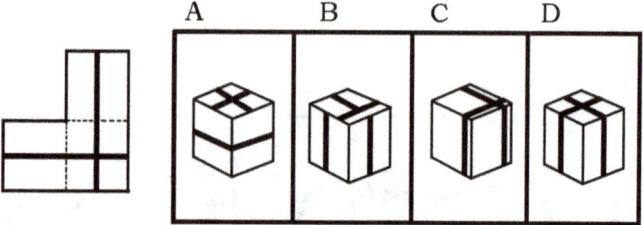

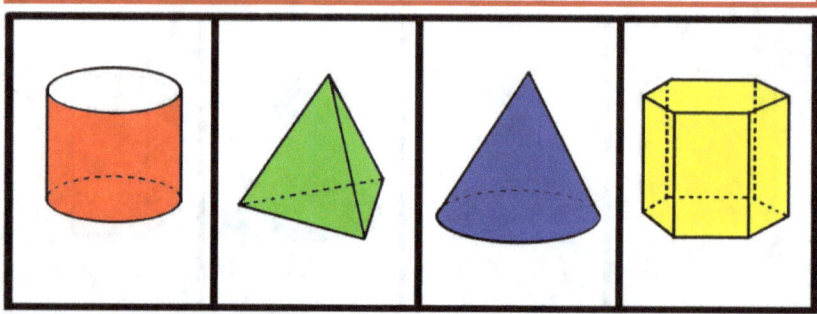

13. When folded into a loop, what will the strip of paper look like?

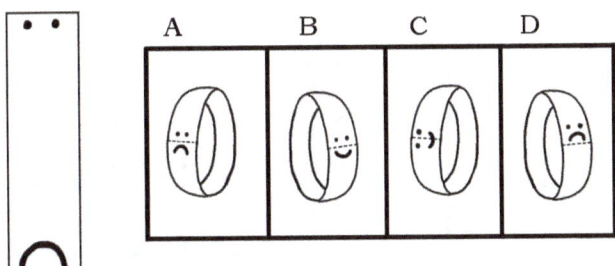

14. Which of the choices is the same pattern at a different angle?

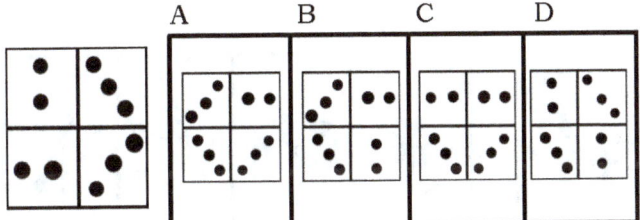

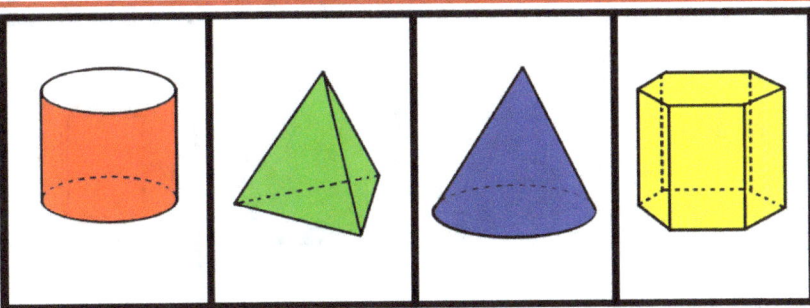

15. When folded along the dotted lines, which shape will you get?

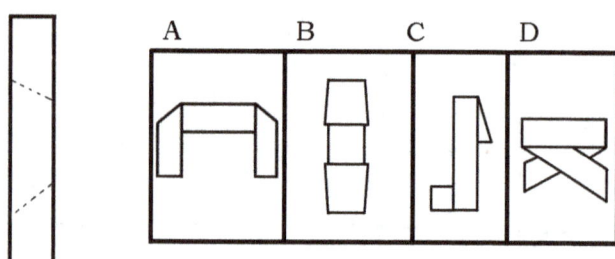

16. When folded, what pattern is possible?

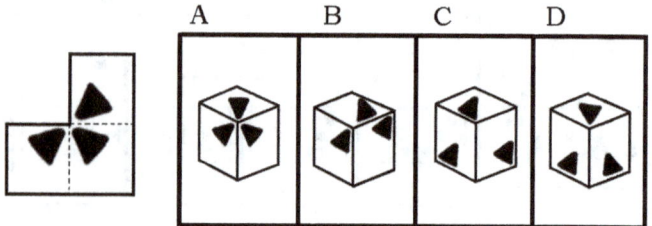

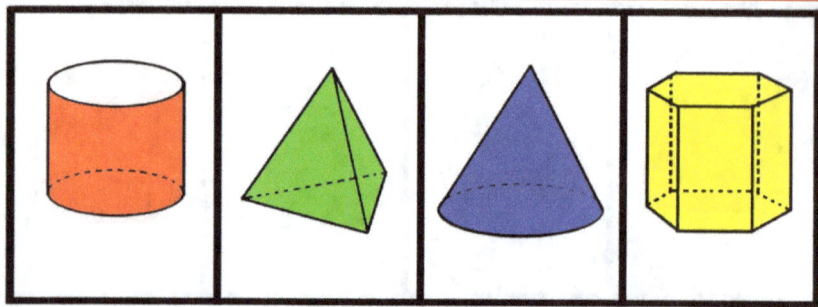

17. When folded into a loop, what will the strip of paper look like?

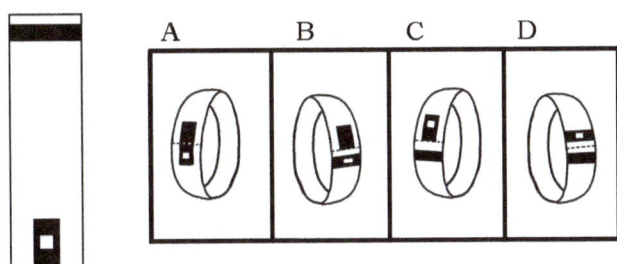

18. Which of the choices is the same pattern at a different angle?

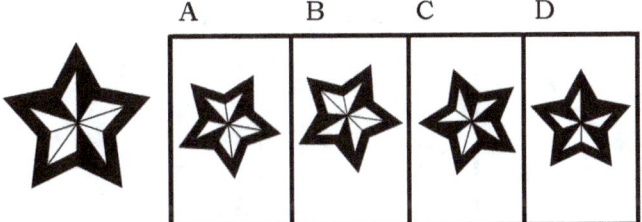

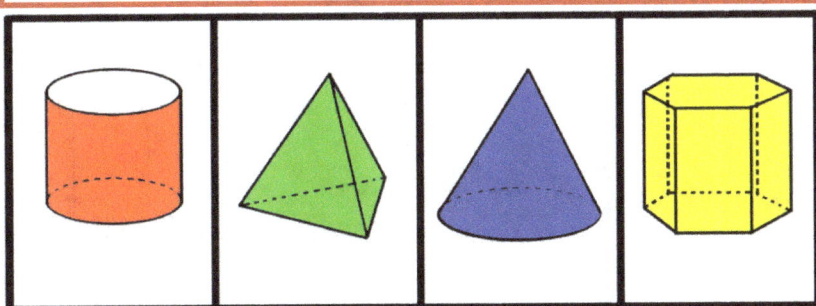

19. When folded along the dotted line, which shape will you get?

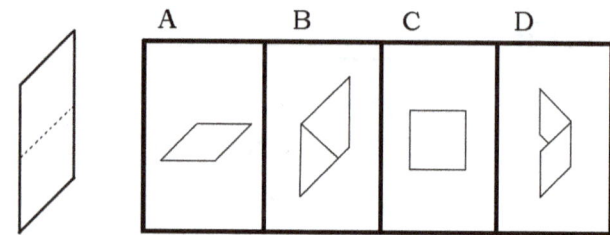

20. When folded, what pattern is possible?

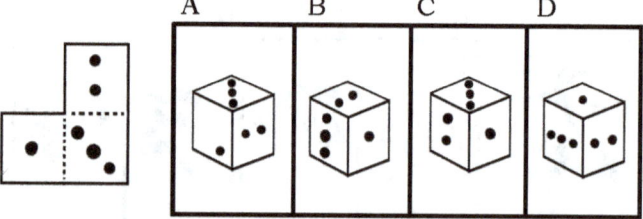

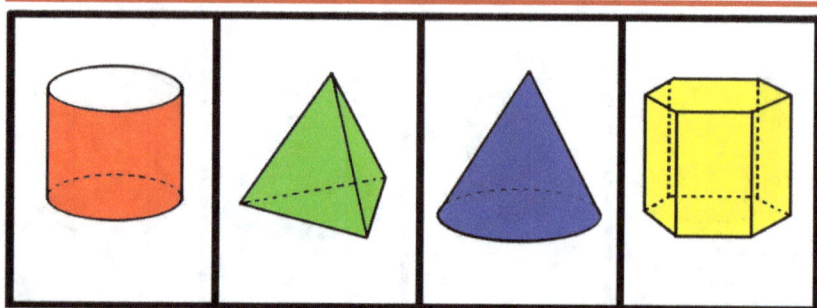

Answer Key

1. D
2. A
3. C
4. B
5. B
6. C
7. B
8. A
9. A
10. A
11. B
12. D
13. B
14. B
15. A
16. A
17. C
18. B
19. D
20. C

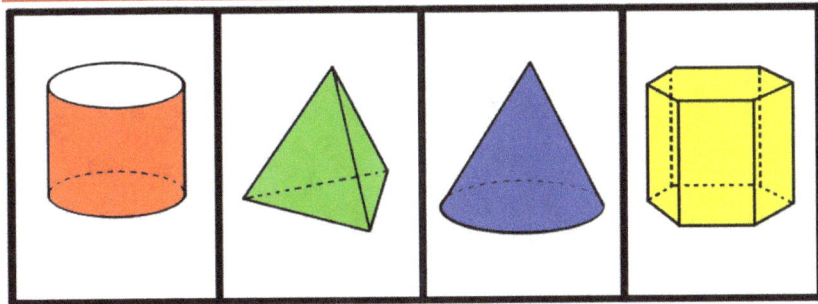

Folding Quiz 2 Answer Sheet

	A	B	C	D
1	○	○	○	○
2	○	○	○	○
3	○	○	○	○
4	○	○	○	○
5	○	○	○	○
6	○	○	○	○
7	○	○	○	○
8	○	○	○	○
9	○	○	○	○
10	○	○	○	○
11	○	○	○	○
12	○	○	○	○
13	○	○	○	○
14	○	○	○	○
15	○	○	○	○
16	○	○	○	○
17	○	○	○	○
18	○	○	○	○
19	○	○	○	○
20	○	○	○	○

1. When folded along the dotted lines, which shape will you get?

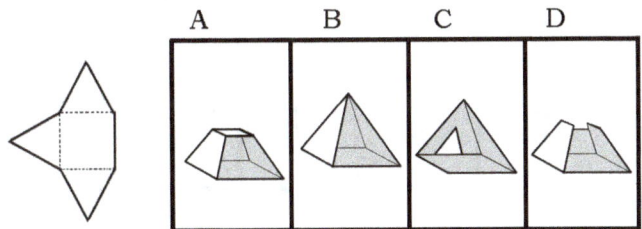

2. When folded, what pattern is possible?

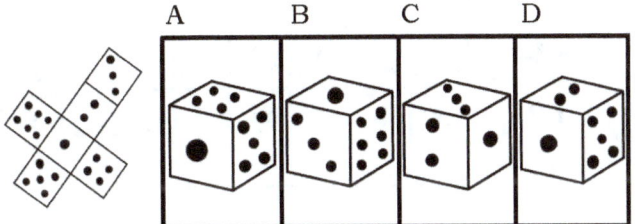

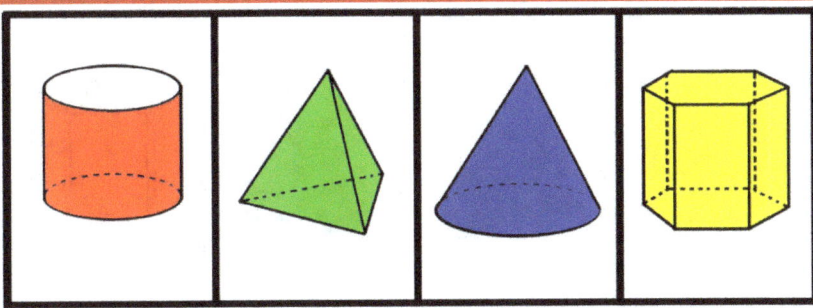

3. When folded into a loop, what will the strip of paper look like?

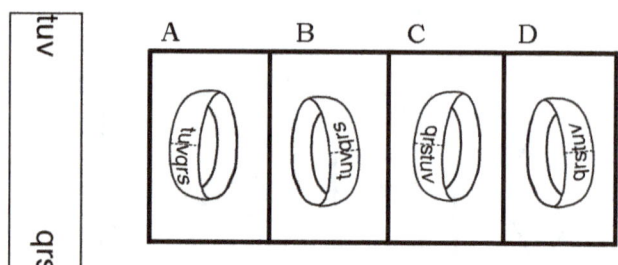

4. Which of the choices is the same pattern at a different angle?

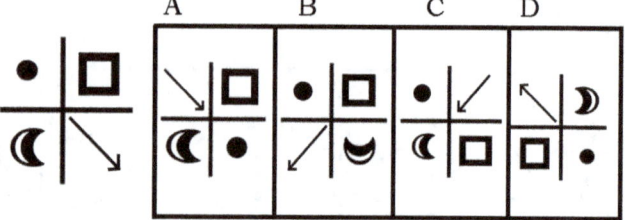

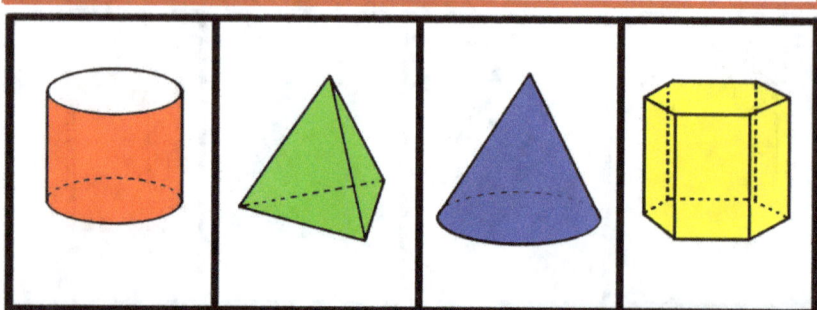

5. When put together, what 3-dimensional shape will you get?

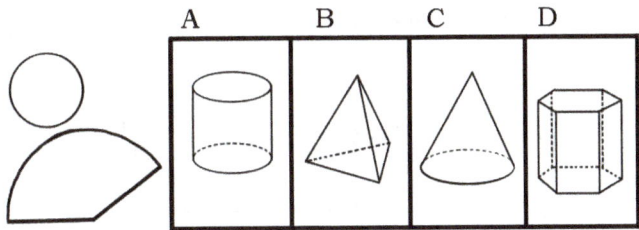

6. When folded, what pattern is possible?

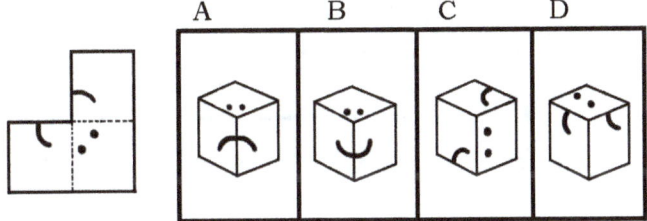

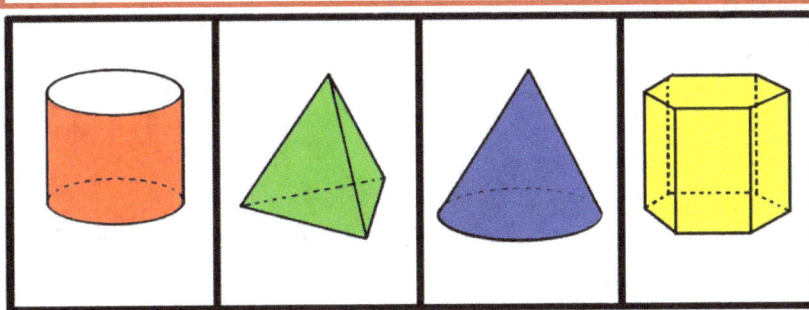

7. When folded, what pattern is possible?

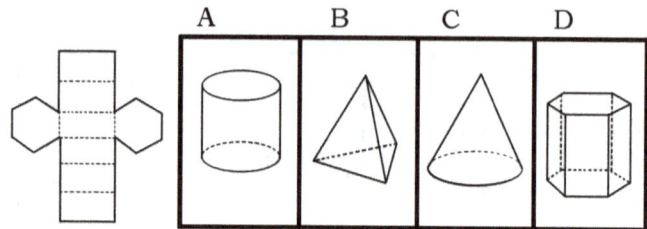

8. Which of the choices is the same pattern at a different angle?

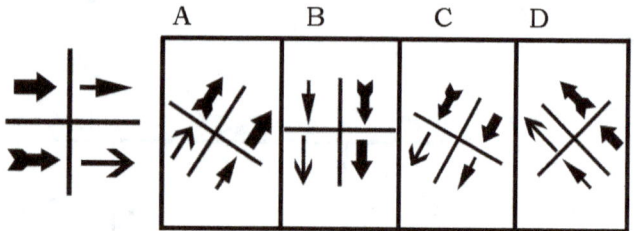

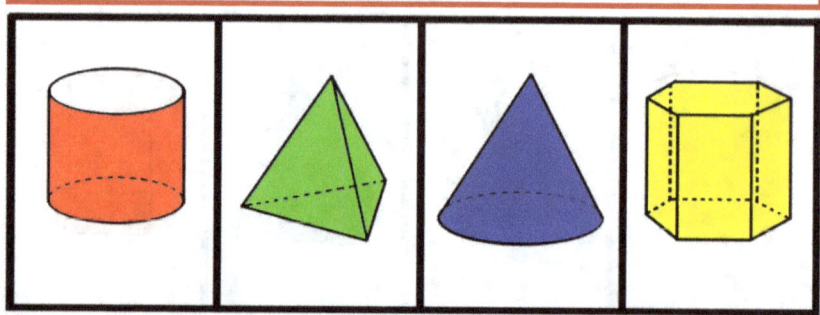

Folding

9. When put together, what 3-dimensional shape will you get?

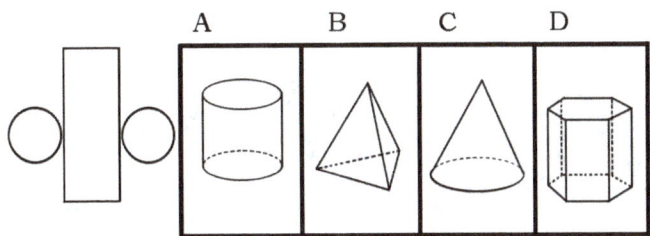

10. When folded into a loop, what will the strip of paper look like?

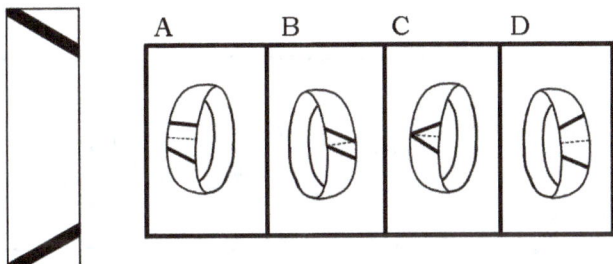

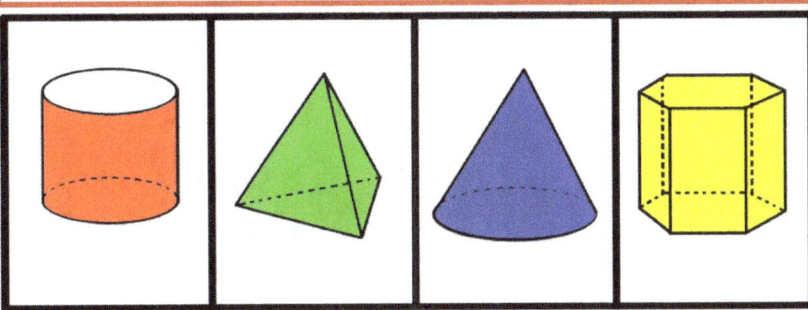

11. Which of the choices is the same pattern at a different angle?

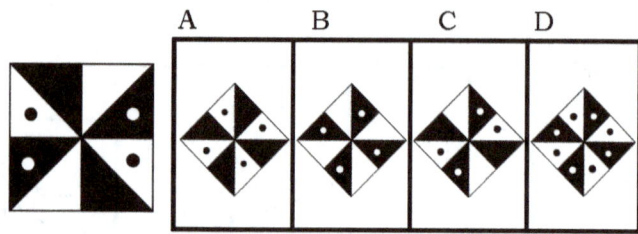

12. When put together, what 3-dimensional shape will you get?

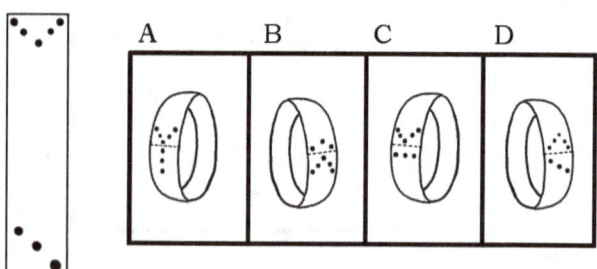

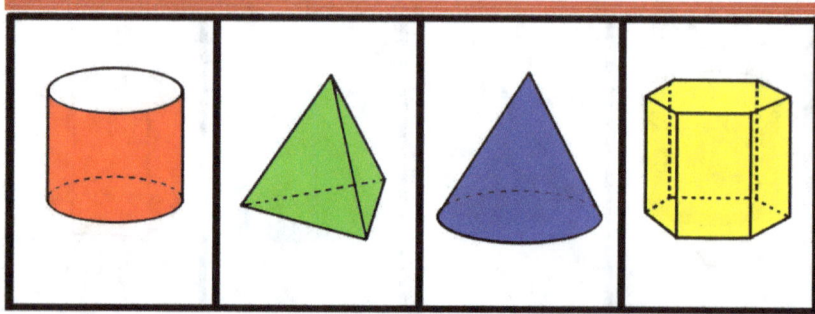

Folding

13. When folded into a loop, what will the strip of paper look like?

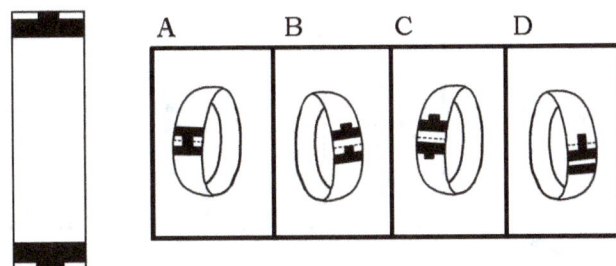

14. Which of the choices is the same pattern at a different angle?

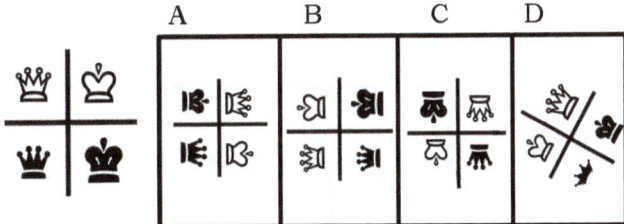

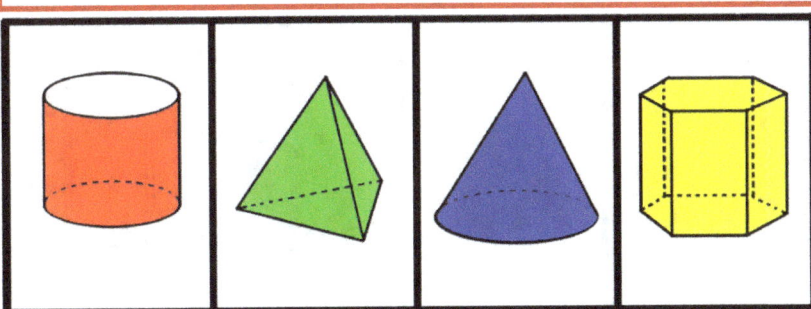

15. When folded into a loop, what will the strip of paper look like?

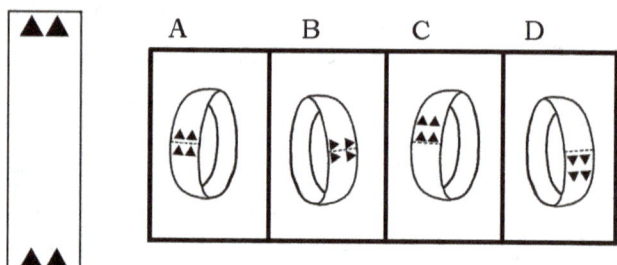

16. When folded, what pattern is possible?

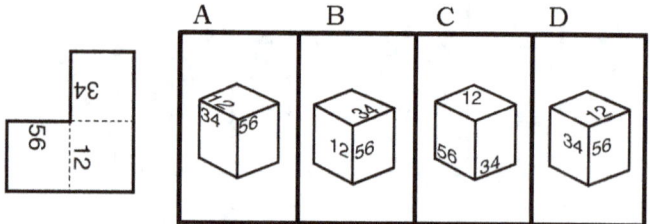

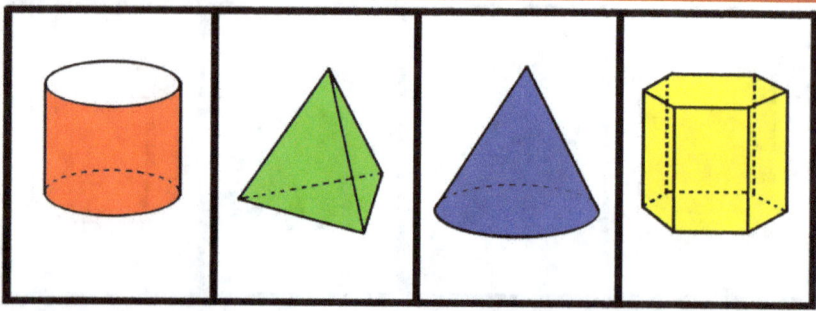

17. When folded into a loop, what will the strip of paper look like?

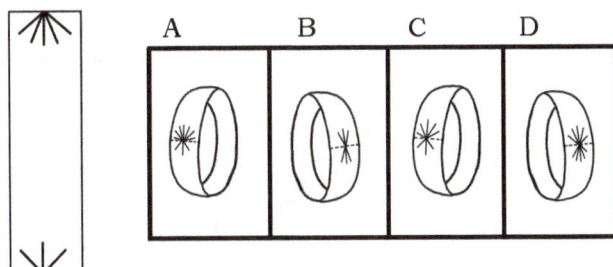

18. Which of the choices is the same pattern at a different angle?

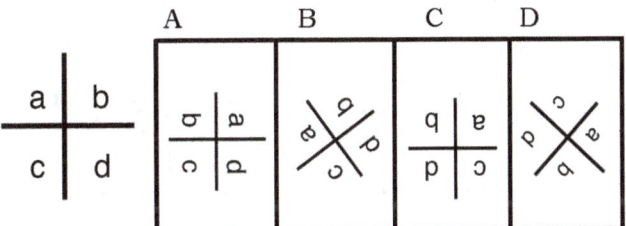

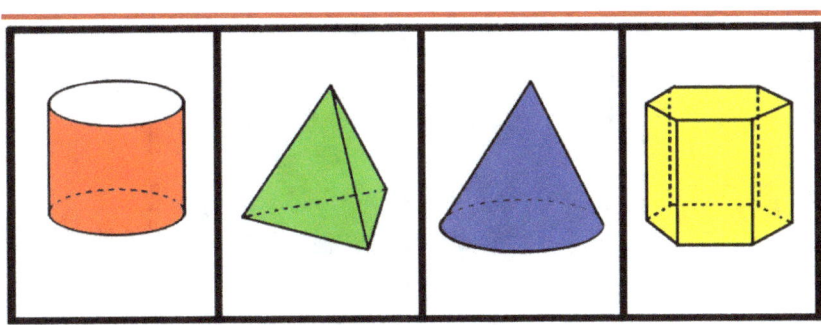

19. When folded, what pattern is possible?

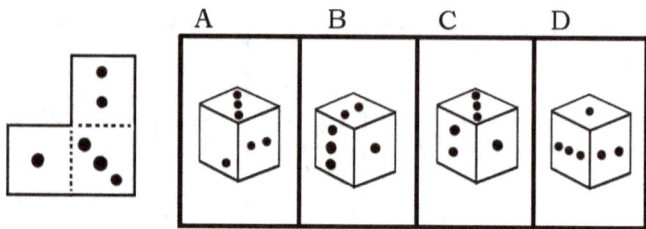

20. Which of the choices is the same pattern at a different angle?

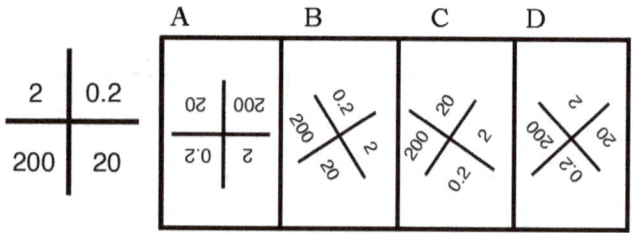

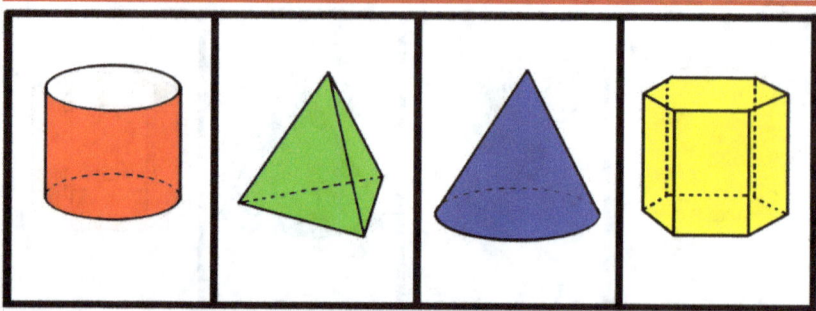

ANSWER KEY

1. B
2. A
3. D
4. D
5. C
6. B
7. D
8. C
9. A
10. C
11. C
12. D
13. A
14. B
15. A
16. D
17. C
18. D
19. C
20. A

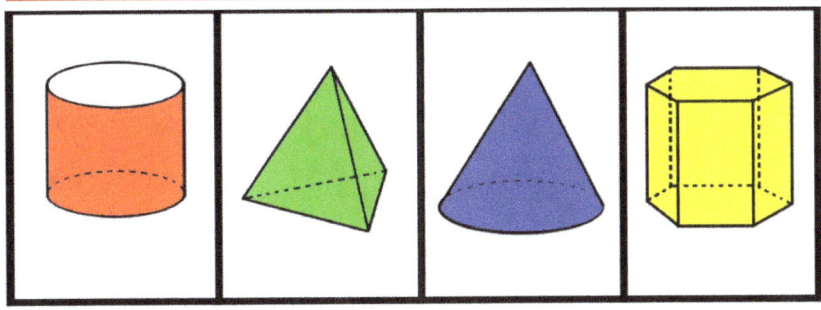

Non Verbal - Figure Matrix

Figure Matrices questions involve patterns of shapes, lines, or symbols arranged in a grid. The grid has two or three rows and tow or three columns, with one of the spaces empty. The task is to figure out the pattern or relationship between the shapes in the rows or columns and choose the correct answer to complete the grid.

These questions test your ability to spot patterns, understand how shapes change, and think logically. For example, shapes might get bigger, rotate, change colors, or follow a sequence as you move across the grid.

Instructions

Look at the Rows and Columns Carefully

Each row or column follows a specific rule or pattern. Start by looking at how the shapes, sizes, colors, or positions change from one box to the next.

Find the Pattern

Ask yourself

- Do the shapes change size or rotate?
- Is there a sequence in colors or the number of shapes?
- Are shapes being added or removed?

Look for rules that are the same across the rows.

Focus on the Missing Spot

Once you understand the pattern, think about what the missing box should look like. Use the rules you discovered to figure out the answer.

Check the Choices

Look at the answer choices provided. Compare them to the pattern and eliminate the ones that don't match.

Take Your Time and Double-Check

If you're not sure, review the pattern again to see if you missed anything. Sometimes, the answer becomes clearer when you look at the problem a second time.

Answer Sheet

	A	B	C	D
1	○	○	○	○
2	○	○	○	○
3	○	○	○	○
4	○	○	○	○
5	○	○	○	○
6	○	○	○	○
7	○	○	○	○
8	○	○	○	○
9	○	○	○	○
10	○	○	○	○
11	○	○	○	○
12	○	○	○	○
13	○	○	○	○
14	○	○	○	○
15	○	○	○	○
16	○	○	○	○
17	○	○	○	○
18	○	○	○	○
19	○	○	○	○
20	○	○	○	○

Select the figure with the same relationship.

1.

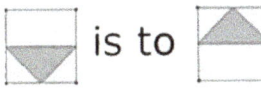

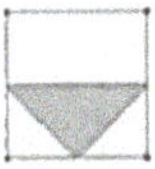 is to 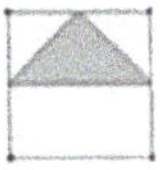

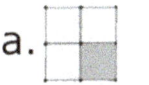

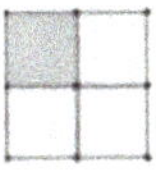 is to ?

a.  b. 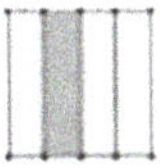

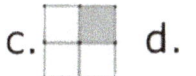

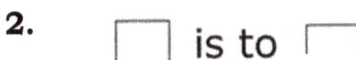

c.  d. 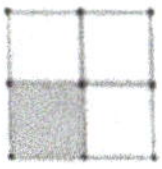

2.

 is to 

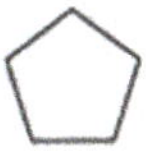 is to ?

a. 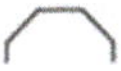 b. 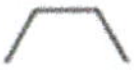

c. 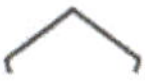 d. 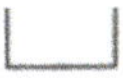

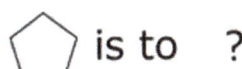

3. 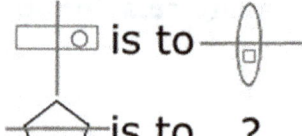 is to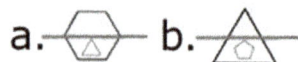

 is to ?

a. 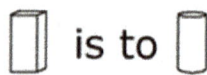 b.

c. d.

4. is to

 is to ?

a. b.

5.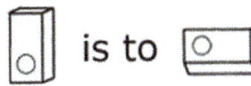

is to ?

a. b.

c. d.

6.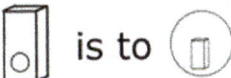

is to ?

a. b.

c. d.

7.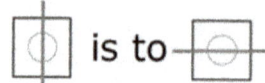

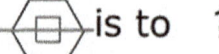 is to ?

8.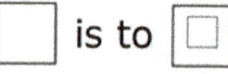

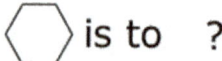 is to ?

9. is to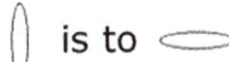

 is to ?

a.   b.

c.   d.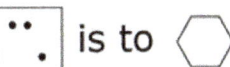

10. is to

 is to ?

a.   b.

c.   d.

11. 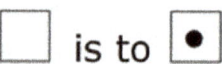
 is to ?

a. b.

c. 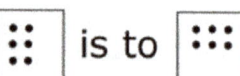 d.

12.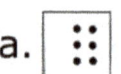
 is to ?

a. b.

c. d.

13.

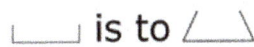

a. 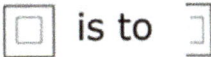 b.

c.   d.

14.

 is to

 is to ?

a.   b.

c.   d.

15. ☐ is to ⌐

   ⬠ is to ?

   a.)   b. ⌐

   c.)   d. ⌐

16. ⬠ is to ⬠

   △ is to ?

   a. ▽   b. ◁

   c. ▷   d. ▭

17.

△ is to ▷

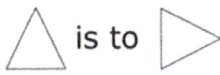 is to ?

a. ◁ b. ▢

c. ⬠ d.

18.

▢ is to △

△ is to ?

a. △ b. ▢

c. ⬠ d.

19.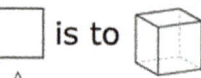

△ is to ?

a. △ b. 🔺

c. ⬠ d. ⌷

20. ⬠ is to ⬡

⬡ is to ?

a. ☐ b. ○

c. ⬠ d. ⬡

Answer Key

1. D
The relationship is the same figure flipped vertically, so the best choice is D.

2. C
The relation is the same figure with the bottom half removed.

3. D
The first pair is a rectangle with a circle inside and then an oval with a square inside. The given figures in the second pair has a triangle inside, so the match will be the circle with a square inside.

4. B
The relation is two upright figures in the first set, and 2 horizontal figures in the second set.

5. C
The first pair contains a box with a circle inside, and the same figure on its side.

6. C
The inside and larger shapes are reversed.

7. D
The relation is the same figure rotated.

8. D
The larger figure has a smaller version inside.

9. D
The relation is the same figure rotated to the right.

10. B
The relation is the number of dots is one-half the number of sides.

11. C
The pattern is the same figure with a dot inside.

12. A
The figure rotates clockwise.

13. B
The relation is the bottom half of the figure.

14. C
The relation is the right half of the first object.

15. B
The relation is the right half of the first object.

16. A
The relation is the same figure rotated.

17. D
The relation is the same figure rotated.

18. B
The relation is a 3-dimensional figure to a 2-dimensional figure.

19. B
The relation is a 2-dimensional figure to a 3-dimensional figure.

20. B
The relation is a n-sided figure to an n + 1 sided figure.

Number Analogies

The Number Analogies section assesses a child's ability to understand numerical relationships and patterns. This section is part of the quantitative reasoning skills tested in the CCAT, which are crucial for solving problems involving numbers and mathematical concepts.

In this section, children are presented with a series of number pairs that have a specific relationship. They are then asked to identify the number that completes a second pair, following the same relationship.

This skill is essential for developing strong mathematical reasoning and problem-solving abilities.

1. Understand the Relationship: Carefully examine the first pair of numbers to understand the relationship between them. It could be addition, subtraction, multiplication, division, or a more complex pattern.

2. Apply the Same Relationship: Once you identify the relationship in the first pair, apply the same relationship to the second pair to find the missing number.

3. Practice Basic Math Operations: Ensure you are comfortable with basic math operations like addition, subtraction, multiplication, and division, as these are commonly used in number analogies.

4. Look for Patterns: Sometimes, the relationship between numbers involves patterns, such as doubling, halving, or following a sequence. Recognize these patterns to solve the analogy.

5. Use Elimination: This is the best strategy for any multiple choice test. If you are unsure of the answer, use the process of elimination to narrow down the choices. Eliminate the options that do not fit the identified relationship.

6. Check Your Work: After selecting an answer, double-check to ensure that the relationship holds true for both pairs of numbers.

Quiz Answer Sheet

	A	B	C	D	E		A	B	C	D	E
1	○	○	○	○	○	21	○	○	○	○	○
2	○	○	○	○	○	22	○	○	○	○	○
3	○	○	○	○	○	23	○	○	○	○	○
4	○	○	○	○	○	24	○	○	○	○	○
5	○	○	○	○	○	25	○	○	○	○	○
6	○	○	○	○	○	26	○	○	○	○	○
7	○	○	○	○	○	27	○	○	○	○	○
8	○	○	○	○	○	28	○	○	○	○	○
9	○	○	○	○	○	29	○	○	○	○	○
10	○	○	○	○	○	30	○	○	○	○	○
11	○	○	○	○	○						
12	○	○	○	○	○						
13	○	○	○	○	○						
14	○	○	○	○	○						
15	○	○	○	○	○						
16	○	○	○	○	○						
17	○	○	○	○	○						
18	○	○	○	○	○						
19	○	○	○	○	○						
20	○	○	○	○	○						

1. If 5 is like a thumb, what is like a pinky?

    a. 5   b. 1   c. 10   d. 6

2. If 6 is like a cookie, what is like half a cookie?

    a. 3   b. 2   c. 4   d. 12

3. If 10 is like a bag, what is like half the bag?

    a. 5   b. 15   c. 20   d. 10

4. Complete the number analogy: 3 is to 6 as 4 is to ?

    a. 8   b. 10   c. 6   d. 5

5. 20 is to 40 as 7 is to __.

    a. 10 b. 14 c. 21 d. 28

6. Find the missing number in the analogy: 5 is to 25 as 7 is to ?

    a. 35 b. 49 c. 18 d. 14

7. If 9 is to 3, then 15 is to ?

    a. 6 b. 4 c. 5 d. 8

8. Choose the correct analogy: 12 is to dozen as 60 is to ?

    a. half dozen b. dozen

    c. five dozen d. two dozen

9. 5 is to 10 as 3 is to ___.

    a. 6   b. 9

    c. 12   d. 15

10. 9 is to 27 as 6 is to ___.

    a. 12   b. 18

    c. 24   d. 36

11. 15 is to 45 as 12 is to ___.

    a. 20   b. 24

    c. 36   d. 36

12. Complete the number analogy:
2 : 1 :: 8 : ?

    a. 2   b. 4

    c. 10   d. 12

13. Fill in the blank:
4 : 1/2 :: 40 : ?

    a. 2   b. 4

    c. 10   d. 5

14. What completes the analogy:
1 : 1/4 :: 8 : ?

    a. 1   b. 2

    c. 3   d. 4

15. Choose the correct answer:
10 : 5 :: 50 : ?

    a. 14   b. 25

    c. 20   d. 24

16. Find the missing number:
1/2 : 2 :: 1/4 : ?

    a. 4   b. 6

    c. 1   d. 12

17. 25 is to 15 as 50 is to __?

    a. 25   b. 30

    c. 35   d. 40

18. 3 is to 18 as 10 is to __?

    a. 60   b. 80

    c. 120   d. 150

19. 10 is to 1 as 30 is to __?

    a. 12   b. 9

    c. 3   d. 27

20. 2 is to 16 as 10 is to __?

    a. 20   b. 40

    c. 15   d. 80

Number Analogies

21. 9 is to 27 as 15 is to __?

    a. 45   b. 38

    c. 36   d. 30

22. 25 is to 50 as 3 is to ?

    a. 5   b. 9

    c. 15   d. 6

23. 3 is to 18 as 10 is to ?

    a. 50   b. 20

    c. 60   d. 30

24. 10 is to 2 as 20 is to ?

    a. 12   b. 8

    c. 16   d. 4

25. 2 is to 16 as 9 is to ?

    a. 12   b. 25

    c. 72   d. 27

26. 9 is to 27 as 25 is to ?

    a. 75   b. 50

    c. 30   d. 90

27. 20 is to 4 as 40 is to ?

    a. 5   b. 8

    c. 10   d. 6

28. 3 is to 9 as 5 is to ?

    a. 15   b. 10

    c. 3   d. 6

29. 1/2 is to 1/4 as 4 is to ?

    a. 2   b. 1

    c. 8   d. 16

30. 2 is to 50 as 5 is to ?

    a. 10   b. 12

    c. 125   d. 25

Answer Key

1. B
When you count fingers, the pinky comes next after the thumb. Hence, the answer is 1.

2. A
Half of a cookie would be like having only one part of the original cookie, which is 3.

3. A
Half of the bag would be like having only one part of the original bag, which is 5.

4. A
The analogy is based on doubling the initial number. So, 3 x 2 = 6, and similarly, 4 x 2 = 8.

5. B
The correct answer is 28. In this analogy, each number is multiplied by 2. So, 7 x 2 = 14.

6. A
This analogy involves squaring the initial number. 5 X 5 = 25, and 7 X 5 = 35.

7. C
In this analogy, the initial number is divided by 3 to get the result. 9 / 3 = 3. Following the same pattern, 15 / 3 = 5.

8. C
A dozen represents 12, so five dozen would be 5 x 12 = 60.

9. A
The correct answer is 6. In this analogy, each number is multiplied by 2. So, 3 x 2 = 6.

10. B
The correct answer is 18. In this analogy, each number is multiplied by 3. So, 6 x 3 = 18.

11. C
The correct answer is 36. In this analogy, each number is multiplied by 3. So, 12 x 3 = 36.

12. B
The pattern is: 2 / 2 = 1. Therefore, 8 / 2 = 4.

13. D
The relation is: 4 / 8 = 1/2. So, 40 / 8 = 5.

14. B
Following the pattern: 1 / 4 = 1/4. So, 8 x 1/4 = 2.

15. B
By applying the pattern: 10 / 2 = 5.
Then, 50 / 2 = 25.

16. C
The relationship is: 1/2 x 4 = 2. Thus, 1/4 x 4 = 1.

17. D
In the first pair, 15 is 10 less than 25. Applying the same logic to the second pair, 40 is 10 less than 50.

18. A
The relationship between 3 and 18 is 6 times. Following this pattern, 10 times 6 equals 60.

19. C
In the given analogy, 1 is 10 / 10 . Following the same logic, 30 / 10 is 3.

20. D
In the initial pair, 2 X 8 is 16. Applying the same ratio, 10 is 8 times less than 80.

21. A
The relation between 9 and 27 is that 27 is 3 times 9. Following this pattern, 15 times 3 equals 45.

22. D
The correct answer is 6. This analogy follows the pattern of multiplying the first number by 2 to get the second number.

23. C
The correct answer is 60. This analogy follows the pattern of multiplying the first number by 6 to get the second number.

24. D
The correct answer is 4. This analogy follows the pattern of dividing the first number by 5 to get the second number.

25. C
The correct answer is 72. This analogy follows the pattern of multiplying the first number by 8 to get the second number.

26. A
The correct answer is 75. This analogy follows the pattern of multiplying the first number by 3 to get the second number.

27. B
The relationship between 20 and 4 is division by 5 (20 ÷ 5 = 4). Following the same pattern, 40 ÷ 5 = 8.

28. A
The relationship between 3 and 9 is multiplication by 3 (3 x 3 = 9). Following the same pattern, 5 x 3 = 15.

29. A
The relationship between 1/2 and 1/4 is division by 2 (1/2 ÷ 2 = 1/4). Following the same pattern, 4 ÷ 2 = 2.

30. C
The relationship between 2 and 50 is multiplication by 25 (2 x 25 = 50). Following the same pattern, 5 x 25 = 125.

Number Series

The CCAT Number Series section evaluates your ability to identify patterns and logical rules in sequences of numbers or letters. In this section, you will be presented with a series of numbers or letters and your task is to determine the next item in the sequence based on the pattern.

This section tests your numerical reasoning skills and your ability to quickly recognize and apply mathematical rule

How to Answer Number Series Questions

1. First, Identify the Pattern: Look for common patterns such as addition, subtraction, multiplication, division, or a combination of these. Sometimes the pattern might involve alternating sequences or more complex mathematical operations.

2. Write Down Differences: If the pattern isn't immediately obvious, write down the differences between consecutive numbers. This can help you spot a consistent change or pattern.

3. Familiarize with Common Patterns: The practice questions below will help you to recognize common number series patterns, such as arithmetic sequences (where the difference between numbers is constant), geometric sequences (where each number is multiplied by a constant), and others.

4. Use Elimination: This is the most powerful multiple choice strategy for any test. Rule out unlikely options. This can help narrow down the possible answers.

Answer Sheet

	A	B	C	D
1	○	○	○	○
2	○	○	○	○
3	○	○	○	○
4	○	○	○	○
5	○	○	○	○
6	○	○	○	○
7	○	○	○	○
8	○	○	○	○
9	○	○	○	○
10	○	○	○	○
11	○	○	○	○
12	○	○	○	○
13	○	○	○	○
14	○	○	○	○
15	○	○	○	○
16	○	○	○	○
17	○	○	○	○
18	○	○	○	○
19	○	○	○	○
20	○	○	○	○

Quiz 1

1. Consider the following sequence: 6, 12, 24, 48, ... What number should come next?

    a. 48   b. 64

    c. 60   d. 96

2. Consider the following sequence: 5, 6, 11, 17, ... What number should come next?

    a. 28   b. 34

    c. 36   d. 27

3. Consider the following sequence: 26, 21, ..., 11, 6. What is the missing number?

    a. 27   b. 23

    c. 16   d. 29

4. Consider the following sequence: L, O, R, ..., Y What is the missing letter?

    a. S   b. U

    c. T   d. M

5. Consider the following sequence: X, Z, B, D, ... What number should come next?

    a. E   b. F

    c. G   d. H

6. Consider the sequence in row A compared to row B. What is the missing number?

| A | 5 | 20 | 100 | 3 | 24 |
| B | 20 | 80 | 400 | 12 | ? |

    a. 96   b. 48

    c. 64   d. 66

7. Consider the following sequence: L, N, P, R, ... What letter should come next?

    a. S   b. T

    c. U   d. V

8. Consider the following sequence: M, P, S,   , Y. What is the missing letter?

    a. V   b. T

    c. U   d. X

9. Consider the following sequence:

  ???

a.    b.    c.

10. Consider the following sequence:

\+ * + * | * + * + | * * + * | + + __ __

    a. + *   b. * *
    c. + +   d. * +

11. Consider the following sequence: 64, 50, 38, 28, 20, ... Find the first three terms.

    a. 15, 10, 5   b. 14, 10, 8
    c. 10, 0, -10   d. 12, 4, -6

12. 2 4 8 16 | 5 10 20 40 |
4 8 16 32 | 3 6 ... 24

   a. 4   b. 12
   c. 8   d. 10

13. Consider the following sequence:
10, 13, 16, 19, ...   What 3 numbers should come next?

   a. 21, 23, 25   b. 21, 24, 27
   c. 22, 25, 28   d. 23, 26, 29

14. Consider Box A and the relationship to the numbers in Box B. What is the missing number in Box B?

Box A

8	12
5	9

Box B

19	27
13	?

a. 18   b. 21
c. 24   d. 14

15. Consider the following sequence: 8, 11, 9, 12, 10, 13, ... What number should come next?

    a. 11   b. 10
    c. 15   d. 16

16. Consider the following sequence: 2, 1, (1/2), (1/4), ... What number should come next?

    a. 1/3   b. 1/8
    c. 1/16   d. 2/8

17. Consider the following sequence: 10, 20, 40, 80, ... What number should come next?

    a. 150   b. 120
    c. 90   d. 160

18. Consider the following sequence: 18395, 18295, 18195, 18095, ... What number should come next?

    a. 18000   b. 18950

    c. 17995   d. 17905

19. Consider the following sequence: -45, -39, -33, -27, ... What number should come next?

    a. 21   b. -21

    c. -25   d. 25

20. Consider the following sequence: ..., ..., 20, 32, 44, 56, 68. Find the first two terms.

    a. -4, 8   b. 0, 12

    c. -6, 8   d. 2, 8

Answer Key

1. D
The numbers doubles each time.

2. A
Each number is the sum of the previous two numbers

3. C
The numbers decrease by 5 each time.

4. B
There are two letters missing between each one, so U is next.

5. B
Miss a letter each time and 'loop' back, so F is next.

6. A
The number in row B is 4 times the number in row A.

7. B
One letter is missing after each letter.

8. A
Two letters are missing after each letter.

9. B
The sequence shifts to the left each time, so the next figure will be the circle.

10. D
Each time the * and + alternate, either singly or doubles.

11. B
The sequence decreases by 2 less each time.
64 --> 50   14
50 -> 38   12
38 -> 28   10
28 -> 20   8
20 --> 14   6
14 -> 10   4

12. B
The numbers double each time.

13. B
The number increase by 3 each time

14. B
The numbers in Box B are the result of (number in Box A * 2)+ 3. So the missing number is 21.

15. A
The sequence increases initially and then decreases in the next term. The relationship between each increase is +3 and the relationship with the alternate decrease is -3. So the answer is -2 from the last given term. 13 − 2 = 11.

16. B
The sequence is decreasing by half. So half of 1/4 = 1/8

17. D
The sequence is increasing. Each new term is obtained by multiplying the last term by 2. Therefore, 80 x 2 = 160

18. C
Each new term is calculated by subtracting 100 from the last term. So, 18095 – 100 = 17995

19. B
Each new term is calculated by adding 6 to the last term, therefore, -27 + 6 = -21

20. A
The sequence is increasing by 12. To find first two terms, we solve backwards by subtracting 12.

Number Series Quiz 2
Answer Sheet

A B C D
1 ○○○○
2 ○○○○
3 ○○○○
4 ○○○○
5 ○○○○
6 ○○○○
7 ○○○○
8 ○○○○
9 ○○○○
10 ○○○○
11 ○○○○
12 ○○○○
13 ○○○○
14 ○○○○
15 ○○○○
16 ○○○○
17 ○○○○
18 ○○○○
19 ○○○○
20 ○○○○

1. Consider the following sequence: 3, 5, 10, 12, 24, ... What 2 numbers should come next?

    a. 48, 58   b. 26, 28

    c. 48, 50   d. 26, 52

2. Consider the following sequence: 1000, 992, 984, 976, ... What 2 numbers should come next?

    a. 968, 961   b. 967, 960

    c. 968, 960   d. 970, 964

3. Consider the following sequence: 0.1, 0.3, 0.9, 2.7, ... What 2 numbers should come next?

a. -8.1, -24.3   b. 8.1, 24.3

c. 5.4, 10.8   d. -5.4, -10.8

4. Consider the following sequence: 32, 16, 8, 4, ... What 3 numbers should come next?

a. 2, 1, 0.5   b. 2, 0, -2

c. 0, -4, -8   d. 2, 1, 0

5. Consider the following sequence: 3, ..., 9, 12, 15. What is the missing number?

    a. 4   b. 7

    c. 6   d. 5

6. Consider the following sequence: 1132, 1121, ... , 1199, ... What number comes next?

    a. 1109   b. 1188

    c. 1189   d. 1180

7. Consider the following sequence: 95, 90, ..., 80, 75. What is the missing number?

    a. 87   b. 85

    c. 86   d. 80

8. Consider the following sequence: ..., 75, 65, 60, 50, 45, 35, ... What 2 numbers are missing?

    a. 70, 35   b. 65, 35

    c. 80, 30   d. 65, 30

9. Consider the following sequence: 91, 85, ..., ..., 67, 61. What 2 numbers are missing?

    a. 81, 71   b. 78, 72

    c. 80, 70   d. 79, 73

10. Consider the following sequence: ..., ..., 120, 129, 138, 147. Find the first two terms.

    a. 102, 111   b. 100, 110

    c. 102, 112   d. 99, 111

11. Consider the following sequence: ..., 95, 88, 93, 86, 91, ... What 2 numbers are missing?

    a. 88, 98   b. 90, 98

    c. 100, 84   d. 90, 84

12. Consider the following sequence: 76, 64, 54, 46, ..., 36, ..., . What 2 numbers are missing?

    a. 40, 32   b. 40, 34

    c. 42, 30   d. 42, 32

13. Consider the following sequence: 3, ..., 12, ..., 48, 96. What 2 numbers are missing?

a. 6, 36

b. 6, 18

c. 8, 16

d. 6, 24

14. Consider the following sequence: 3, 13, 22, 30, 37, ... What number comes next?

a. 45

b. 47

c. 43

d. 42

15. Consider the following sequence: ..., ..., 4, 9, 14, 19. Find the first two terms.

    a. -5, 0   b. 0, 2

    c. -6, -1   d. -5, 0

16. Consider the following sequence: 63, 57, 52, 48, ... What number comes next?

    a. 42   b. 37

    c. 45   d. 40

17. Consider the following sequence: 17, 23, 29, 35, ... What 3 numbers should come next?

a. 41, 47, 54

b. 42, 47, 53

c. 40, 45, 50

d. 41, 47, 53

18. Consider the following sequence: 11, 15, 20, 26, ... What 3 numbers should come next?

a. 31, 37, 42

b. 33, 41, 50

c. 32, 38, 46

d. 36, 46, 56

19. Consider the following sequence: 45, 40, ..., 30, 25. What is the missing number?

    a. 35   b. 38

    c. 33   d. 32

20. Consider the following sequence: 120, 110, ..., 90, 80. What is the missing number?

    a. 95   b. 100

    c. 105   d. 115

Answer Key

1. D
The sequence is increasing by adding 2 and multiplying 2 alternately. The next 2 terms are 24 + 2= 26 and 26 x 2 = 52.

2. C
The sequence is decreasing by 8.

3. B
The sequence is increasing by multiplying each the last term by 3. 2.7 x 3= 8.1 and 8.1 x 3 = 24.3

4. A
The sequence is decreasing by dividing the last term by 2.

5. C
The sequence is increasing by +3.

6. B
The sequence is reducing by 11.

7. B
The sequence is decreasing by +5.

8. C
The sequence is decreasing by -5 and -10 alternately; the first term is 75 – 5 = 70 and the last term is 35 – 10= 30.

9. D
The sequence is increasing by +6.

10. A
The sequence is increasing by +9.

11. D
The sequence is increasing and decreasing alternately. It increases by +5 and decreases by -7. The first term will thus be the second term 95 – 5 = 90 and the last term will be 91 – 7 = 84.

12. B
The difference between the terms starts from 12 and decreases by 2 i.e. 12, 10,8,6,4,2. The missing terms are 46 – 6=40 and 34 – 0 =34

13. D
Each term is being doubled or multiplied by 2 to get the next term. 3 x 2 = 6 and 12 x 2 = 24.

14. C
The sequence increase by 1 less each time.
3 + 10 = 13
13 + 9 = 22
22 + 8 = 30
30+ 7 = 37

15. D
The sequence increases by 5 each time.

16. C
The sequence decreases by 1 less each time
63 - 6 = 57
57 - 5 = 52
52 - 4 = 48

17. D
The sequence increases by 6 each time.

18. B
The sequence increases by +1 each time
11 + 4 = 15
15 + 5 = 20
20 + 6 = 26
26 + 7 = 33
33 + 8 = 41
41 + 9 = 50

19. A
The sequence decreases by 5 each time. So, the missing number is 45 - 5 - 5 = 35.

20. B
The sequence decreases by 10 each time. So, the missing number is 120 - 10 - 10 = 100.

NUMBER PUZZLES

In this section, students are presented with a puzzles that involve numbers and simple equations, where one item is missing.

Number puzzles help young learners develop their mathematical thinking in a fun and interactive way.

Answer Sheet

	A	B	C	D	E		A	B	C	D	E
1	○	○	○	○	○	21	○	○	○	○	○
2	○	○	○	○	○	22	○	○	○	○	○
3	○	○	○	○	○	23	○	○	○	○	○
4	○	○	○	○	○	24	○	○	○	○	○
5	○	○	○	○	○	25	○	○	○	○	○
6	○	○	○	○	○
7	○	○	○	○	○
8	○	○	○	○	○
9	○	○	○	○	○
10	○	○	○	○	○
11	○	○	○	○	○
12	○	○	○	○	○
13	○	○	○	○	○
14	○	○	○	○	○
15	○	○	○	○	○
16	○	○	○	○	○
17	○	○	○	○	○
18	○	○	○	○	○
19	○	○	○	○	○
20	○	○	○	○	○

1. 2 + ___ = 9

    a. 7   b. 3

    c. 6   d. 8

2. (3 X 4) – 5 = ___

    a. 17   b. 7

    c. 12   d. 15

3. (8 X 2) X (2 X 3) = ___

    a. 60   b. 72

    c. 96   d. 92

4. ___ + (6 * 7) = 43

    a. 5   b. 2

    c. 9   d. 1

5. 7 + (3 X ___) = 28

    a. 7   b. 4

    c. 6   d. 10

6. 8 - ? = 3

    a. 2   b. 3

    c. 5   d. 8

7. What number is missing in the equation: 5 + ? = 12?

    a. 3   b. 6

    c. 7   d. 8

8. What number is missing in the equation: 9 - ? = 3?

    a. 4   b. 5

    c. 6   d. 7

9. What number is missing in the equation: 4 x ? = 16?

    a. 2   b. 3

    c. 4   d. 5

10. What number is missing in the equation: 14 ÷ ? = 7?

    a. 1   b. 2

    c. 3   d. 4

11. What number is missing in the equation: 10 + ? = 15?

    a. 3   b. 4

    c. 5   d. 6

12. 4 x ? = 16

    a. 2   b. 4

    c. 6   d. 8

13. 12 ÷ ? = 3

    a. 2   b. 3

    c. 4   d. 6

14. ? + 7 = 15

    a. 6   b. 8

    c. 9   d. 10

15. If 5 + ? = 8, what is the missing number?

    a. 2   b. 3

    c. 4   d. 5

16. If 10 - ? = 6, what is the missing number?

    a. 3   b. 4

    c. 6   d. 8

17. Complete the pattern: 2, 4, 6, ?, 10

    a. 7   b. 8

    c. 9   d. 11

18. If 18 ÷ ? = 3, what is the missing number?

    a. 3   b. 4

    c. 5   d. 6

19. What number completes the equation: 5 + ? = 12?

    a. 4   b. 6

    c. 7   d. 8

20. What is the missing number in the equation: 15 - ? = 9?

    a. 4   b. 5

    c. 6   d. 7

21. What number is missing in the equation: 8 x ? = 32?

    a. 3   b. 4

    c. 5   d. 6

22. Complete the equation: ? ÷ 4 = 5

    a. 15   b. 16

    c. 17   d. 18

23. Find the missing number: 27 / ? = 9

    a. 2   b. 3

    c. 4   d. 5

24. If 8 - ? = 3, what should replace the question mark?

    a. 4   b. 5

    c. 6   d. 7

25. What is the missing number in the equation: 6 x 3 = ?

    a. 12   b. 15

    c. 18   d. 21

Answer Key

1. A
2. B
3. B
4. D
5. A
6. A
7. D
8. B
9. C
10. A
11. C
12. D
13. B
14. C
15. B
16. B
17. A
18. C
19. C
20. A
21. B
22. A
23. B
24. A
25. B

After Taking a Practice Test

What to do after you take a practice test

- Go through your answers carefully. For each wrong answer, refer to the explanation, and work through the questions step-by-step.

- What kind of question (e.g. analogies, sentence completion etc.)

- Look for patterns in your incorrect answers – what is it exactly that you are doing wrong or don't understand.

- What types of questions do you have the most difficulty with? Refer to the tutorials and try to understand the questions.

Getting the Most from Practice Questions

Taking a practice test is probably the best way to prepare for a test.

Quick tips to get the most from practice questions:

Simulate Test Conditions

- Choose a quiet, distraction-free environment.

- Use a timer and allow just under 1 minute per question.

- Avoid using notes or online texts while doing practice questions

Take it seriously -

- Treat the practice test as if it's the real exam -

- Familiarize yourself with the format and topics - this will reduce anxiety.

Practice questions come in varying degrees of difficulty, ranging from basic to advanced levels.

This diversity helps in assessing different aspects of your understanding and skills. To handle these effectively, start by thoroughly reading each question to understand what is being asked. For easier questions, focus on accuracy and speed. For more challenging ones, break them down into smaller parts and tackle each part methodically.

Remember, staying calm and confident is key to successfully navigating through questions of all difficulty levels.

After Completing a Practice Test

Reviewing your work after you take a practice test is critical.

Immediate Review

- Make a note of any questions you found challenging or topics that felt unfamiliar or difficult.

- How was your time management?

- Overall comfort during the test?

Do a Thorough Review

• Go over your answers focusing on correct and incorrect answers.

• For incorrect answers, identify misunderstandings knowledge gaps or problem subject areas - here is where you need to spend your study time.

• **Look for Patterns**

• Look for recurring themes in your errors to pinpoint specific areas needing improvement.

• Assess whether mistakes were due to content gaps, misinterpretation of questions, or time constraints.

Test Preparation Tips

1. Create a Study Schedule:
Set aside a specific time each day for studying. For example, study for 30 minutes after school every day.

2. Use Flashcards:
Write down key facts or vocabulary words on flashcards. Review them regularly.

3. Take Breaks:
Take short breaks during study sessions to stay focused. For example, study for 20 minutes, then take a 5-minute break to stretch or have a snack.

4. Get a Good Night's Sleep:
Make sure to get plenty of rest the night before the test. For example, go to bed early to ensure you are well-rested and alert.

5. Stay Positive and Confident:
Think positive and be confident. For example, remind yourself that you have studied and are prepared for the test.

6. Ask for Help:
If you don't understand something, ask a teacher, parent, or friend for help.

How to Answer Multiple Choice

1. Read the Question Carefully:
Make sure to read the entire question before looking at the answer choices. For example, if the question asks, "What is 5 + 3?" make sure you understand it is asking for the sum of 5 and 3.

2. Look at All the Answer Choices:
Read all the answer choices before selecting one. For example, if the choices are 6, 7, 8, and 9, make sure to consider each one before choosing.

3. Eliminate Wrong Answers:
Cross out the answers you know are incorrect. For example, if you know 5 + 3 is not 6 or 7, eliminate those choices.

4. Use Process of Elimination:
Narrow down your choices by eliminating the wrong answers. For example, if you are left with 8 and 9, think about which one makes the most sense.

5. Look for Clues in the Question:
Sometimes the question itself can give you hints about the correct answer. For example, if the question asks about a "sum," you know it is asking for an addition problem.

6. Double-Check Your Work:
If you have time, go back and review your answers. For example, make sure you didn't make a simple mistake like adding incorrectly.

7. Stay Calm and Focused:
Take deep breaths and stay calm. For example, if you feel nervous, take a moment to relax before answering the next question.

8. Trust Your First Instinct:
Often, your first choice is the correct one. For example, if you initially think the answer is 8, go with that unless you find a reason to change it.

9. Don't Leave Any Questions Blank:
If you are unsure, make your best guess. For example, if you don't know the answer, choose the one that seems most likely.

Conclusion

Congratulations! You have made it this far because you have applied yourself diligently to practicing for the exam and no doubt improved your potential score considerably! Getting into a good school is a huge step in a journey that might be challenging at times but will be many times more rewarding and fulfilling. That is why being prepared is so important.

Study then Practice and then Succeed!

Good Luck!

www.ingramcontent.com/pod-product-compliance
Lightning Source LLC
Chambersburg PA
CBHW072154070526
44585CB00015B/1141